THE HOUSE OF MIRTH

A Novel of Admonition

TWAYNE'S MASTERWORK STUDIES
Robert Lecker, General Editor

THE HOUSE OF MIRTH

A Novel of Admonition

LINDA WAGNER-MARTIN

TWAYNE PUBLISHERS • BOSTON
A Division of G. K. Hall & Co.

The House of Mirth: A Novel of Admonition
Linda Wagner-Martin

Twayne's Masterwork Studies No. 52

Copyright 1990 by Linda Wagner-Martin
All rights reserved.
Published by Twayne Publishers
A division of G. K. Hall & Co.
70 Lincoln Street
Boston, Massachusetts 02111

Copyediting supervised by Barbara Sutton.
Book production by Janet Z. Reynolds.
Typeset by Compositors Corporation, Cedar Rapids, Iowa.

Printed on permanent/durable acid-free paper
and bound in the United States of America.

First published 1990.
10 9 8 7 6 5 4 3 2 1 (hc)
10 9 8 7 6 5 4 3 2 1 (pb)

Library of Congress Cataloging-in-Publication Data

Wagner-Martin, Linda.
    The house of Mirth : a novel of admonition / Linda Wagner-Martin.
        p.   cm. — (Twayne's masterwork studies ; no. 52)
    Includes bibliographical references.
    ISBN 0-8057-9433-6 (alk. paper). — ISBN 0-8057-8135-8 (pbk. :
alk. paper)
    1. Wharton, Edith, 1862-1937. House of mirth.   I. Title.
II. Series.
PS3545.H16H688   1990
813'.52—dc20   90-30430
                                                                        CIP

For Margaret Petrak

Contents

Note on the References and Acknowledgments
Chronology: Edith Wharton's Life and Works

1.	Historical Context	1
2.	The Importance of the Work	5
3.	Critical Reception	8

a reading

4.	Narrative Voice	15
5.	The Character of Lily Bart	22
6.	The Structure	30
7.	The Mother-Daughter Paradigm	41
8.	Story as Subtext	49
9.	The Impossible Suitors	58
10.	Daisy Miller and The House of Mirth	66
11.	Edith Wharton and The House of Mirth	77

Notes   89
Bibliography   93
Index   101

Note on the References and Acknowledgments

References to *The House of Mirth* throughout this text are from the Penguin edition of 1985.

I am indebted throughout this study to the work of Elizabeth Ammons, Margaret McDowell, and Cynthia Griffin Wolff. Many thanks to the Beinecke Library, Yale University, for permission to reproduce the photograph of Edith Wharton; and to the Harry Ransom Humanities Research Center, University of Texas at Austin, for allowing me to quote from Wharton's letters.

Edith Wharton, circa 1911, Wharton Archive.
Used by permission of the Yale University Library, New Haven, Connecticut.

Chronology:
Edith Wharton's Life and Works

1862	Edith Newbold Jones born 24 January in New York City to George F. and Lucretia Stevens Rhinelander Jones.
1866–1872	Travels in Europe with family.
1872–1879	Winters in New York, summers in Newport, R.I. Edith's nicknames ("Sweet," "Lily," "Puss," and "John") reflect the many dimensions of her personality. Writes novella *Fast and Loose* in 1876–77. Her mother publishes Edith's *Verses* in 1878, and William Dean Howells publishes one of those poems in *Atlantic Monthly* in 1879 (Edith's book is sent to him by Longfellow).
1879	Edith's Fifth Avenue debut.
1880	The most "social" of Edith's seasons, with the attention of Harry Stevens, which continued through 1882, despite his mother's objections.
1880–1882	Because of George Jones' failing health, the family travels in France and Italy until Jones' death in the spring of 1882.
1882	Edith's engagement to Stevens announced in August. It is broken off in late October.
1883	Edith meets Walter Berry at Bar Harbor in July, but he leaves at the close of the season without proposing. She also meets Teddy Wharton, a Bostonian.
1885	Teddy and Edith are married 29 April (Lucretia Jones omitted Edith's name from the wedding invitations, an ominous sign of her daughter's relative importance).
1885–1888	The Whartons travel, spending springs in Italy and living in Pencraig and Land's End, Newport. Edith calls their three-month Aegean yacht cruise in 1888 "the crown of my youth."

	She inherits a bequest valued at half a million dollars after taxes from a distant cousin.
1889	The Whartons live in New York where Edith resumes writing. She publishes poems and a sketch in *Scribner's*.
1891	Wharton writes "The Fullness of Life," a bitter allegorical story about marriage.
1892	She completes her long novella, *The Bunner Sisters*.
1894	After three years of intermittent depression, Wharton breaks down. Her illness interrupts what is becoming important literary activity, and developing friendships. She is treated by a colleague of neurologist S. Weir Mitchell's.
1897	Wharton, working with Ogden Codman, publishes *The Decoration of Houses*.
1898	Wharton ill during winter; in the spring she visits Walter Berry in Washington. Consults with S. Weir Mitchell.
1899	*The Greater Inclination* (stories) published.
1900	*The Touchstone* published. Wharton's illness and depression continue.
1901	Wharton builds The Mount in Lenox, Massachusetts, and finds great solace in that project and in living there. *Crucial Instances* (stories) published.
1902	*The Valley of Decision* published. Wharton experiences another breakdown in February. After spending several years writing for the stage, she publishes her translation of Hermann Sudermann's *Es Lebe das Leben*. Meets Henry James.
1903	*Sanctuary* published. Teddy Wharton's breakdown.
1904	*The Descent of Man and Other Stories* and *Italian Villas and Their Gardens* published.
1905	*Italian Backgrounds* and *The House of Mirth* published, to great celebrity.
1907	Wharton publishes *Madam de Treymes, The Greater Inclination,* and *The Fruit of the Tree*. The Whartons move their winter home from New York to 58 Rue de Varenne, Paris. Wharton meets Morton Fullerton.
1908	Wharton visits Henry James in London; affair with Fullerton begins. *The Hermit and the Wild Woman* and *A Motor-Flight through France* (based on her tour of France with Henry James and her husband, Teddy) published.
1909	Publishes *Artemis to Actaeon;* moves to 53 Rue de Varenne in

the Faubourg Saint-Germain section of Paris, where she lives until 1920.

1910   Teddy's further breakdown, with disclosure of his embezzlement and affairs. *Tales of Men and Ghosts* published; Fullerton affair intermittent.

1911   Separates from Teddy Wharton, who has sold The Mount. *Ethan Frome* published.

1912   *The Reef* published.

1913   *The Custom of the Country* published. Divorces Teddy. Travels in Germany with Bernard Berenson.

1914   Travels to Algiers and Tunis with Percy Lubbock and Gaillard Lapsley, and to Majorca with Walter Berry. Organized war relief in Paris.

1915   *Fighting France* published. Wharton contributes to war relief efforts.

1916   *The Book of the Homeless* and *Xingo and Other Stories* published. Wharton in charge of 600 Belgian orphans. Henry James dies.

1917   Wharton awarded the Order of Leopold, Belgium, and the French Legion of Honor. *Summer* published.

1918   Buys Pavillon Calombe in a village near Paris. Publishes *The Marne.*

1919   *French Ways and Their Meaning* published.

1920   Wharton restores medieval monastery at Hyères on the Riviera for a summer home; she publishes *The Age of Innocence* and *In Morocco.*

1921   Wharton awarded the Pulitzer Prize in fiction for *The Age of Innocence.*

1922   *The Glimpses of the Moon* published. Screenplay adaptation written by F. Scott Fitzgerald.

1923   Wharton the first woman to be awarded the Doctor of Letters degree at Yale University; this is her only trip to America after 1912. *A Son at the Front* published.

1924   Wharton awarded the Gold Medal for fiction by the National Institute of Arts and Letters. *Old New York* published.

1925   *The Mother's Recompense* and *The Writing of Fiction* published.

1926   Wharton elected to the National Institute of Arts and Letters. She takes a yacht trip on the Aegean, meaning to recapture the golden days of the 1888 cruise. *Here and Beyond* (stories) and *Twelve Poems* published.

1927 Walter Berry dies. *Twilight Sleep* published.

1928 Teddy Wharton dies. *The Children* published.

1929 Wharton's serious illness. *Hudson River Bracketed* published.

1930 Wharton elected to the American Academy of Arts and Letters. *Certain People* (stories) published.

1932 *The Gods Arrive* published.

1933 *Human Nature* (stories) published.

1934 *A Backward Glance,* Wharton's autobiography, published.

1936 *The World Over* (stories) published.

1937 *Ghosts* (stories) published. Wharton dies 11 August following a stroke. She is buried at Versailles next to the ashes of Walter Berry. Her papers are left to Yale University, with all publication withheld until 1968. The important biographies and critical studies published since then have benefited from the Yale collection.

1938 *The Buccaneers* published.

one

Historical Context

The New Woman was a harbinger of change—in family life and culture, as well as in women's existences—and it is about the turn-of-the century New Woman that much of Edith Wharton's fiction revolves. Wharton herself was a product of many of the conflicts that the women's movement had set off. She had to face the issues of what an appropriate life for a woman should be, and to decide for herself whether or not to marry and bear children; whether she should have a career or profession, or become the social butterfly her society preferred. Naturally, Wharton's fiction would show her interest in the possibilities for changes in women's lives in the twentieth century.

In both England and the United States, many women were dissatisfied with their roles during the later part of the nineteenth century. Women of wealth wanted more than to be "protected," but "the long, golden Edwardian garden-party"—with its emphasis on women as beautiful, innocent objects, the desirable icons of an acquisitive patriarchal culture—only reinforced the idea that women needed to be taken care of.[1] The image of women as delicate flowers—too fragile to play sports, study, or earn a living—was a stereotype that had little to do with women's abilities. Their rancor at being suffocated and diminished under the

1

guise of some necessary male shelter had been simmering long before Ibsen's 1879 *A Doll's House* or Kate Chopin's more shocking 1899 *The Awakening*. In those controversial literary works, strong women characters chose to leave the comfort of protective security to find existences of their own. When Chopin's Edna Pontellier chooses to die rather than live that life of "piety, purity, submissiveness and domesticity,"[2] many readers were horrified at her willfulness and boycotted Chopin's writing.

Patriarchal control of women's lives during the nineteenth century was not only economic, it was also religious and sexual. The economic control was clear in men's amassing of immense fortunes, and in the gilded-age emphasis on the display of great wealth. According to both the Bible and the nineteenth-century church, women were to marry and be ideal helpmeets for their husbands and True Woman families. The True Woman was sexually naive and pure; virginity was a requirement for any socially approved marriage, and the course of a woman's life was to be self-sacrifice for the good of the family unit. Men, stereotyped by society as less pure and more sexual, could indulge whatever baser sexual appetites they had through appropriate channels (i.e., women of lower class or nonwhite race). In forming what became known as the "double standard of behavior," society recognized that men could do whatever they wanted in relation to women; after all, they controlled all economic power. A common text for sermons during the nineteenth century was the role and duties of the "good" woman. Male physicians became specialists in women's mental health, as well as obstetrics and gynecology.[3] The message was clear: everything that touched a woman's life was in the control of the patriarchy.

Beginning with comments by Harriet Martineau and Sarah Grimke (including the latter's in *Letters on the Equality of the Sexes and the Condition of Women* in 1838), women writers such as Margaret Fuller, Lucretia Mott, and Elizabeth Cady Stanton presented arguments not only for women's right to vote, but also for improved educational opportunities, psychological and economic freedom, and the right of women to exercise choice about their lives. The Declaration of Sentiments and Resolutions issued at the Seneca Falls Convention in 1848 was a touchstone document, and momentum from that meeting continued—despite the Civil War—as women drove for social reforms and the vote. Charlotte Perkins Gilman's 1898 text, *Women and Economics,* was so important to the controversy surrounding the role of women in society that Gertrude Stein quoted from it in a speech in Baltimore several years later. Questions about the power of religion to undermine women's physical and psychological freedoms, about ownership of property and wealth, and about women's role in marriage were all threatening to the dominant male culture.

At the International Council of Women in 1888, Elizabeth Cady Stanton noted that, while women did not have the vote, other positive changes had occurred since the early 1800s. If women in 1838 were—as Stanton said—"bond slaves," by 1888 they had access to 563 institutions of higher education, and more than 35,000 female students were enrolled there. Women workers comprised 17 percent of the labor force, amounting to some four million employees by 1890. Most of those women worked at low-paying jobs, but by 1886, 390 women physicians were practicing medicine in twenty-six states. Women were excluded from practicing law in some states, but they could become ministers and professors, architects and scientists.[4]

Such statistical gains, of course, only created more pressure for women choosing to pursue the path of the New Woman instead of following the preference of the culture—and often of their families—and becoming the True Woman. Public opinion was aroused, and the anger of a society that felt insecure as the result of changes in family structure and women's behavior showed itself in satirical cartoons and vindictive essays. When Edith Wharton (née Edith Jones) as an adolescent began to consider becoming a professional writer, her fashionable mother moved up her debut by a year. Expending her energy learning to become a high-society True Woman left Edith little time to explore her possible career as a writer, and that passion was submerged for more than twenty years.[5]

Wharton creates in *The House of Mirth* the impressionable character of Lily Bart, flowerlike in fragility as well as name, who has accepted the social decree that she become a beautiful marriageable object. Wharton's ironic choice in the novel of having Lily be twenty-nine years old at the time of the narrative, instead of nineteen as a reader might expect, allows her to question the wisdom of Lily Bart's having followed the dictates of her society. As Wharton's protagonist moves from one bad choice to the next, she maintains her virginity and her virtue; but society chooses to blind itself to her purity. Instead, Lily Bart becomes a defamed—and damaged—object of art. As her last chances for marriage falter, the reader is made to question relentlessly the ethics of Lily's seemingly protective society. *The House of Mirth* has nothing about it that is pleasant or comic, and as Wharton draws her condemnatory fiction to its inevitable close, the reader is forced to recognize the dangers of a woman's rebellion against the cultural mandates of True Womanhood.

two

The Importance of the Work

Wharton's *The House of Mirth,* serialized in *Scribner's* from January to November of 1905, was officially published as a novel on 14 October of that year. The novel had the most rapid sales of any of Scribner's books to that time and rivaled or surpassed the other best-sellers of the year, Upton Sinclair's *The Jungle,* Thomas Dixon's *The Clansman,* and Robert Smythe Hichans's *The Garden of Allah.* It clearly met a demand in American readers that had gone unsatisfied. The poignant but all-too-real narrative of the beautiful Lily Bart, fast aging beyond marriageability, could be read in a number of ways (some conventional, others more subversive). *The House of Mirth* appeared midway in a pattern of writing that explored themes brought to light during the New Woman controversies.

Ibsen's dramas that questioned women's roles in marriage (*A Doll's House,* 1879; *Hedda Gabler,* 1890) and similar world fiction (Flaubert's *Madame Bovary,* 1857; Tolstoy's *Anna Karenina,* 1877; George Eliot's *The Mill on the Floss,* 1860, and *Middlemarch,* 1872; Hardy's *Tess of the D'Urbervilles,* 1891) supplemented the growing American attention to these themes. Post–Civil War American fiction created the American Girl (Henry James's Daisy Miller in the 1879 novella of that title, and in 1881 his Isabel Archer in *The Portrait of a Lady*), the innocent ingenue whose trust traps her in a morass of European intrigue. More to the point, a number of nineteenth-century American women writers were creating fiction that had female heroes: Elizabeth Stuart Phelps Ward's *The Silent Partner*, 1873, and *The Story of Avis*, 1879; Louisa May Alcott's *Work*, 1873; Mary Wilkins Freeman's *A New England Nun*, 1891; Sarah Orne Jewett's *The Country of the Pointed Firs*, 1889; Charlotte Perkins Gilman's "The Yellow Wallpaper," 1892, and *Women and Economics*, 1898; Kate Chopin's *Bayou Folk*, 1894, and *The Awakening*, 1899.

Readers, though interested in women characters working through what appeared to be real-life dilemmas, could not bear too much reality. The outcry that greeted Chopin's *The Awakening*, with its protagonist's choice of suicide over a life of compromise, was frightening: called "sex fiction," the book effectively marked the end of Chopin's career as novelist.[6] Much the same reception met Theodore Dreiser's comparatively sympathetic treatment of yet another "fallen" (but independent and successful) woman, *Sister Carrie*, published in 1900. The line seemed blurred. Where could the novelist portray women realistically, even in sexual matters, and where would the reader prefer blinders?

Whether conscious of the furor within the literary world, or expressing her own place in the continuum of the New Woman, Wharton managed in *The House of Mirth* to choose strategies that appeased the hostile readers. In her choice of a point of view that told the story with seeming objectivity, Wharton was able to show all sides of Lily Bart's personality—her hesitation as well as her ambition, her scruples as well as her understanding of the games society insisted upon playing. Much of the story is given through the eyes of Lawrence Selden, a character who seems to have Lily's best interests at heart. Selden appears to be a high-minded, philosophical young lawyer, himself weary of the social fabric that would catch and doom Lily. In fact, the novel begins and ends with Selden's comments about Lily, making her the social object—the icon—readers would have expected in a novel of manners. Yet the vitality of the 1905 novel stems largely from the contradictions Wharton was able to incorporate in it. By the end, the reader is not sure that Selden is so admirable—and if he is not, then his authoritative voice should be questioned. When Lily dies, the reader wants some vindication for that death: what has the society paid for its brutal and meaningless vengeance on this woman? By composing a novel that left such important questions unanswered, Wharton foreshadowed the very kind of "open" text the modernists would pride themselves on creating—and the impact of *The House of Mirth,* as well as other of Wharton's fictions, might have been more influential on the younger American modernists than literary history has shown. F. Scott Fitzgerald, for one, was much impressed with Wharton's work.

The House of Mirth, taken with Chopin's *The Awakening* and Gilman's "The Yellow Wallpaper," is a key example of a woman's voice exploring significant women's themes in a covert manner: fiction as disguise. In unraveling the text of Lily Bart's story, through a narrative that appears to be conventional but causes surprising division among its readers, the modern-day reader can recognize the subterfuge women writers needed to employ in order to keep their share of the reading public while expressing potentially unpopular truths.

The House of Mirth provides insight into what Sandra M. Gilbert and Susan Gubar have termed "the anxiety of authorship," the defensiveness and unease women writers experience when they attempt to write stories that focus on human relationships. And it serves as an exciting example of the creation of narrative techniques that allow the expression of an alternate story, as a seeming subtext, under the more apparent plot line of a primary (and perhaps more conventional) text. Learning to read both text and subtext enables today's reader to understand the brilliance, and the subtlety, of women writers' work at the turn of the century.[7]

three

Critical Reception

As one might expect with a best-selling novel by a woman writer in 1905, critical reaction—though usually approving—had an undercurrent of reservation. The tendency to believe that everything written by a woman was "domestic" or "sentimental" was well established by this point in history, as Nina Baym describes in *Novels, Readers, and Reviewers*.[8] That tendency was less apparent in reviews of *The House of Mirth*, however, because of Wharton's established reputation as an "intellectual" writer. The reviews of her 1905 novel primarily continued the positive tone of the reception of her earlier short story collections (*The Greater Inclination*, 1899; *Crucial Instances*, 1901; and *The Descent of Man and Other Stories*, 1904) and longer fictions (*The Touchstone*, 1900; *The Valley of Decision*, 1902; and *Sanctuary*, 1903). That previous work had been praised for its perfection of style and technique, its attention to characters' motivation, and its seriousness, although some critics found Wharton's treatment of moral issues too intellectualized and her characters sometimes remote. *The House of Mirth* was accordingly seen as an advance for Wharton: it was much more complex, much longer, and much more moving than her earlier work, and the character of Lily Bart was undeniably accessible.

Critical Reception

Wharton's protagonist was given high praise. She was described as "complex" and "ill-starred," drawn more fully than any woman character of George Eliot's, and the heroine of a "poignant tragedy." Henry James said of Lily Bart that she was "very big and true—and very difficult to have *kept* big and true."[9] But even as *The House of Mirth* was seen to be Lily's story, that identification led to some disapproval. A few reviewers claimed that unpleasantness was not the province of fiction, that by stressing the "sordid" Wharton did not only her work but her readers a grave disservice ("people rise quicker to a hope" than to unhappiness). The moral purpose of fiction cannot be undermined because of an author's fascination with character. Not all reviewers found Lily Bart poignant or positive. The *Athenaeum* (London) reviewer described her as a woman who needs money; Mary Moss wrote in *Atlantic Monthly* that Lily inspires interest rather than caring; and the London *Saturday Review* described her as "a masterly study of the modern American woman with her coldly corrupt nature and unhealthy charm." Alice Meynell anticipates a somewhat later critical interest in the character of Lawrence Selden, as she finds him—as the spokesman for a "better" world—the important character of the novel.[10]

Throughout the commentary ran the refrain of Wharton's debt to Henry James, though the insistence of that comparison was less obvious in reviews of *The House of Mirth* than it had been in reviews of Wharton's story collections. Her work was also compared with that of Ellen Glasgow, Guy de Maupassant, Booth Tarkington, Howard Sturgis, and George Eliot. Some of this comparison was to privilege Wharton's achievement; some of it worked to limit her accomplishment, as in the blunt *Times Literary Supplement* comment that "Wharton does lack the creative gift at its fullest"—and therefore *The House of Mirth* "is not fiction at its very highest point." Again, an English reviewer has chosen to limit Wharton's success, and it can well be said that American reviewers were, collectively, more enthusiastic about the novel and about Wharton. Perhaps they were better able to understand the fiction and the society it represented; perhaps they were more eager to find American writers who could compete with the English literary figures.[11]

The House of Mirth was recognized both at the time of its original publication and throughout the successive decades of Wharton's writing career as Wharton's breakthrough novel and one of her most important books. In bringing to life the elite New York culture—complete with its villainy and its pride—Wharton found firm ground, much as Sherwood Anderson was to reach in his *Winesburg, Ohio* (1919) and as William Faulkner was to find, at Anderson's urging, in his *Sartoris* (1929). Wharton herself had benefited from the wisdom of Annie Fields and Sarah Orne Jewett, women who cared about the art of fiction and its importance in representing the lives of women characters in authentic, meaningful ways. By placing those women characters in believable contexts, the author could bring value to their daily lives and keep the characterization well above the stereotype of so many fictional characters in turn-of-the-century women's novels. Wharton's aims were complex, and she may not have been entirely conscious of them even as she wrote *The House of Mirth.* Nonetheless, she enjoyed the novel's rapid sale and ubiquitous acclaim, even if she did not realize how important a book it was. In keeping with her usually humble demeanor, she wrote to her publisher Charles Scribner that she had had a new photograph taken for use in the postpublication success of *The House of Mirth,* one "with my eyes down, *trying to look modest.*"[12]

Wharton was always much involved in the criticism of each of her works. She wrote to friends with humility, acerbity, and sometimes glee about this reaction or that. The amazingly rapid sales of *The House of Mirth* brought her what she called "a trunkful" of "funny" letters as well as serious ones, and she illustrated the former in this way: "One lady is so carried away that she writes, 'I love, not every word in the book, but every period and comma.' I hope she meant to insert an 'only' after the 'not.'"[13]

She was also very concerned that readers would misread, as some reviewers had, especially those who objected to the novel on the grounds of its moral lapses or its unpleasantness. In a 5 December 1905 letter to Morgan Dix, rector of Trinity Church in New York, Wharton clarifies her professional commitment, saying that she aims to write fiction "which probes deep enough to get at the relation with the eternal laws." The issue is not "unpleasantness" but whether or not good fiction has as its subject "a criticism of life. . . . *No* novel worth anything can be anything but a novel 'with a purpose.'"[14]

The unprecedented quantity of books and essays published on Wharton's work in the 1970s and 1980s (see Secondary Works in the Bibliography) testifies to the surety of the author's aesthetic vision. She was a writer of great talent and versatility, always mindful of her ethical responsibility to write as well as she could, about subjects of value. Current attention to *The House of Mirth* proves the importance of her first major novel, and underscores the accuracy of Arthur Hobson Quinn's assessment that, in the 1920s, Wharton was "the foremost living novelist writing in the English language." As Quinn asked then, "which of *us* are as truly alive as Lily Bart, as Ethan Frome, as Ellen Olenska, as May Welland? And which of us will live as long?"[15] There is little question that Edith Wharton is now recognized as a major American writer, and *The House of Mirth,* correspondingly, as a major American novel.

a reading

four

Narrative Voice

Wharton's choice of narrative voice is in some ways the most traditional decision she made in writing *The House of Mirth*. Most nineteenth-century fiction was written from a third-person omniscient perspective. Wharton's elegant, mannered, and somewhat ironic voice was what readers in 1905 would have expected. Yet the voice itself is, finally, not omniscient. It is sharply curtailed by Wharton's choice of focus. It tells the reader only certain things, about certain people.

At the beginning of the novel—and at intervals throughout, including the ending—the voice assumes the vantage point of the mind of Lawrence Selden, the figure Wharton uses as both observer and suitor.

> Selden paused in surprise. In the afternoon rush of the Grand Central Station his eyes had been refreshed by the sight of Miss Lily Bart.
>
> It was a Monday in early September, and he was returning to his work from a hurried dip into the country; but what was Miss Bart doing in town at that season? If she had appeared to be catching a train, he might have inferred that he had come on her in the act of transition between one and another of the country-houses which disputed her presence after the close of the Newport season; but her desultory air perplexed him. She stood apart from the crowd, letting it drift by

her. . . . There was nothing new about Lily Bart, yet he could never see her without a faint movement of interest: it was characteristic of her that she always roused speculation, that her simplest acts seemed the result of far-reaching intentions.[16]

Rather than omniscient, and supposedly impartial, narration, here Wharton gives the reader the opinions of a man who is never objective about Lily. Yet to the uninitiated reader, because the language is third-person, this highly selected view will appear to be omniscient.

What Wharton creates, in fact, is the character of Selden as a puzzling, critical narrator, the kind of highly intellectualizing voice most readers privilege. This rare view of Lily, coupled in the following pages with Selden's images of the cost she has taken to evolve into the beauty her society expects her to be, has already shaped the view of the innocent reader. All we know about Lily has come through Selden's eyes, and even when she speaks for herself (with independence and longing, wishing to be able to live as he does), the reader discounts her words because Selden is commenting on them from his third-person perspective.

> "How delicious to have a place like this all to one's self! What a miserable thing it is to be a woman." She leaned back in a luxury of discontent.
>
> Selden was rummaging in a cupboard for the cake.
>
> "Even women," he said, "have been known to enjoy the privileges of a flat."
>
> "Oh, governesses—or widows. But not girls—not poor, miserable, marriageable girls!" . . .
>
> As he watched her hand, polished as a bit of old ivory, with its slender pink nails, and the sapphire bracelet slipping over her wrist, . . . she was so evidently the victim of the civilization which had produced her, that the links of her bracelet seemed like manacles chaining her to her fate. (7)

Wharton's choice of presentation model puts the reader as firmly in the grip of the patriarchal culture as Lily is. Lily's fortune—her very life—will depend on the way the men of her social group "read" her story. Lily's role in society is to marry well. If her possible marriage partners are not convinced of her value, she will not be able to make a successful match. As if to underscore this theme, Wharton keeps the narrative voice trained on Lily in situations that emphasize this role, woman as marriageable object.

Later in book 1, Wharton sets up an essential conversation between Selden and Lily. They are discussing success and Lily begins:

> "Success?" She hesitated. "Why, to get as much as one can out of life, I suppose. It's a relative quality, after all. Isn't that your idea of it?"
>
> "My idea of it? God forbid!" He sat up with sudden energy, resting his elbows on his knees and staring out upon the mellow fields. "My idea of success," he said, "is personal freedom."
>
> "Freedom? Freedom from worries?"
>
> "From everything—from money, from poverty, from ease and anxiety, from all the material accidents. To keep a kind of republic of the spirit—that's what I call success." (68)

Filled with rhetoric we can identify with (of course the reader wants to be free, just as he or she wants Lily to be free), Selden's words are here presented without any context. What the reader needs to know here is what Selden is really saying to Lily. Taken in a vacuum, his words are empty abstractions. (How can either of them be free from worries about money unless money is plentiful?) He evidently assumes that *he* can reach this nirvana and *she* cannot: there is an admonitory tone to his answer, and the vehemence of his "God forbid!" puts her immediately in the wrong. In the most generous interpretation, it sounds as if Selden cares what happens to Lily, as if he wants her to think about what she is doing with her life. At another level, Selden could be playing word games, creating a superiority for himself that he makes Lily understand she has no way of attaining. But the hopeful reader assumes that Selden has ideas of his own about Lily's promise, that his interest in her is more than that of a mere observer.

By choosing to withhold information about Selden's motivation, information the reader could expect if this were a traditional narrative, Wharton creates a dynamic that draws the reader into the same position in reading the novel that Lily Bart is in throughout the narration. Only the male characters in *The House of Mirth* have necessary information.

Just as Selden has sophisticated philosophical understanding, Simon Rosedale has a wide range of business and social acumen, and Dorset and Trenor have financial prowess. Lily understands nothing about any of these subjects. As she says in frustration after Mrs. Peniston's will has been read, when Gerty Farish has said she should not listen to the gossip and innuendo of her friends, "I *must* listen to them; I must know where I stand" (224).

Wharton repeats this pattern at key junctures in the narrative. When Lily is at a turning point, Selden—after a long period of absence—appears, always with advice. Lily listens. Selden's words sound right. They are spoken with conviction. They appear to be, morally, on-target. As does Lily, we admire what Selden says to her—but we are still ignorant of his motivation. When Selden insists that she leave her job as secretary to Norma Hatch, she does ask him directly what she is to do instead. He has no answer, except that Mrs. Hatch's is not the place for her. Lily replies with anger that he has no right to malign Mrs. Hatch, and that he has disappeared when she has needed a friend at numerous times in the past. But she does leave her job, following his injunction. Misleading to both the reader and Lily is Selden's phrasing, "You are to let me take you away from here," wording which implies that he will become her protector. Yet he does not, and he avoids any personal responsibility by saying that he has interfered in this way because it is "simply the universal right of a man to enlighten a woman when he sees her unconsciously placed in a false position" (279–80).

Wharton shows this speech to be a great affront. Selden not only denies personal responsibility in claiming this "universal" right; he continues to make value judgments about Lily, based on little or no accurate information. The movement of the narrative increases the irony of Selden's appearing just now: once Lily gives up her work with Norma Hatch and takes the job as seamstress in the milliner's shop, she begins the final downward spiral. Selden is speaking from the point of view of economic safety. He has money. He assumes that Lily has money, even though she has told him she does not. He gives no credence at all to her words, and discounts her mention of starvation as if she is exaggerating her problem. By this point in the novel, the reader has little sympathy for

Selden's mistakes. Selden refuses to understand Lily, yet his austere and judgmental voice still sounds as the narrator's.

Part of the impact of *The House of Mirth's* narration stems from the fact that Wharton has often given the reader the chance to see how wrong Selden can be. In the house-party scene, Selden seems to think Lily's meeting him is inconsequential; the reader knows that her distant treatment of Percy Gryce, combined with her seeming to take Selden away from Bertha Dorset, leads to her losing any chance of marrying Percy. Yet Selden says, too modestly, "I don't flatter myself that my coming has deflected your course of action by a hair's breadth" (66). At the peak of his love for her, just before he sees her leaving the Trenor house, he thinks complacently, "he would lift her out of it, take her beyond! That *Beyond!* on her letter was like a cry for rescue. . . . Well, he had strength for both—it was her weakness which had put the strength in him" (158–59). As Wharton makes all too clear even in her indirect narrative method, Selden has only the strength of his rhetoric. He very seldom acts—and when he does act, his gesture comes too late.

Much of the narrative does not depend on Selden's point of view, however, because he is so often absent. When the third-person voice is unnamed or unassociated, it is usually acerbic.

Miss Bart was turning to carry the letters upstairs when she heard the opening of the outer door, and her aunt entered the drawing-room. Mrs. Peniston was a small, plump woman with a colourless skin lined with trivial wrinkles. Her grey hair was arranged with precision, and her clothes looked excessively new and yet slightly old-fashioned. They were always black and tightly fitting, with an expensive glitter: she was the kind of woman who wore jet at breakfast. Lily had never seen her when she was not cuirassed in shining black, with small tight boots, and an air of being packed and ready to start; yet she never started.

She looked about the drawing-room with an expression of minute scrutiny. "I saw a streak of light under one of the blinds as I drove up; it's extraordinary that I can never teach that woman to draw them down evenly."

Having corrected the irregularity, she seated herself on one of the glossy purple arm-chairs; Mrs. Peniston always sat on a chair, never in it. (107)

The reader assumes that some description is necessary in any fiction, but this passage conveys more than simple detail about Lily's rich aunt. The emphasis on the "trivial," the precise, the ordered, helps the reader dislike the only relative who has the power, financial as well as social, to help Lily.

Wharton's novels do provide a sense of context. Yet within the matrix of description, the reader is conscious that even background descriptions are highly selected, that the details mentioned casually in a paragraph will come to be essential strings in the unraveling of a character later in the story. Here Mrs. Peniston's icy, sterile propriety will be the reason that she cannot tolerate Lily's apparently casual misbehavior on the Dorset cruise. As a result of Wharton's careful detail, the reader feels that Mrs. Peniston will eventually disinherit Lily with the same gusto with which she straightens the window blind.

Characterization of simple personae—the "flat" characters of any fiction—can be achieved through such external presentations, but the characterization of the complex protagonist is harder to achieve. Many of the third-person descriptive passages of the novel (those which do not voice Selden's thoughts) concern Lily Bart's inner self. Yet because Wharton does not use a first-person voice, does not move outside her third-person omniscient point of view, the reader feels little immediacy in the portrait.

Lily stood motionless, keeping between herself and the char-woman the greatest distance compatible with the need of speaking in low tones. The idea of bargaining for the letters was intolerable to her, but she knew that if she appeared to weaken, Mrs. Haffen would at once increase her original demand.

She could never afterward recall how long the duel lasted, or what was the decisive stroke which finally, after a lapse of time recorded in minutes by the clock, in hours by the precipitate beat of her pulses, put her in possession of the letters; she knew only that the door had finally closed and that she stood alone with the packet in her hand. (106-7)

One of the ironies of Wharton's narrative method is that the reader never bridges the distance between the polysyllabic descriptors, the linked phrases, the long sentences, and the heart of Lily's devastation. Wharton describes Lily's confusion, her self-hatred, her acquiescence to the society that she knows will only undermine her, but the language of the sections of narration that do explore Lily as character is often much less vital than the exploration of character Wharton is undertaking. Only when Lily's anguish is handled in dialogue, so that Lily's voice reaches the reader, does her plight have urgency. Yet because Lily cannot speak candidly to most of the people in the novel—certainly not to Selden or Mrs. Peniston, or to her social friends—those sections are rare. The closest the reader comes to Lily is in the aftermath of her learning that she has inherited only ten thousand dollars. She feels herself disinherited. Gerty, in trying to comfort her, insists that if she would only tell "the whole truth" everything would work out. "'The whole truth?' Miss Bart laughed. 'What is truth? Where a woman is concerned, it's the story that's easiest to believe. In this case it's a great deal easier to believe Bertha Dorset's story than mine, because she has a big house and an opera box, and it's convenient to be on good terms with her." Lily's cynicism is appropriate; the reader has seen the events unravel just as she summarizes. And when Gerty presses her further, to tell her story from the beginning, Lily answers the solipsistic inquiry with impatience. "You asked me just now for the truth—well, the truth about any girl is that once she's talked about she's done for; and the more she explains her case the worse it looks" (226).

Wharton's choice of narrative method seems to provide the reader with all the information necessary to comprehend Lily's story; in effect, however, her method has withheld some information, has misinformed the reader in other cases, and has kept the "whole truth" of Lily's story in the hands, and the voice, of Lawrence Selden. To read *The House of Mirth* is to learn to "read" Selden, Lily, and the matrix of society within which they speak.

five

The Character of Lily Bart

Wharton works hard to make the reader understand how evanescent truth—even "the whole truth"—is. Gerty Farish is the most sympathetic listener imaginable. As a social worker, her profession is listening, and her familiarity with women's misfortunes makes her particularly well suited to be Lily's confidante.

Lily's seeming mockery of Gerty's assurance ("From the beginning? Dear Gerty, how little imagination you good people have!") is less hardhearted than it appears. Lily's answer (or nonanswer) is a symptom of her real insight into the complexity—and the culpability—of language. All her life she has lived among people whose words never convey their real meanings, whose words are intended not to convey meaning but only to serve as counters in the necessary rituals of the various social games. Why should her telling her own story, even "from the beginning," satisfy any need or justify any action?

Lily speaks the truth when she says to Gerty that she does not, herself, know her story. To have a story implies that a narrator (in this case, Lily) has been an actor, has been in charge of living that narrative. The tragedy of Lily's attempts at a story is that it is a non-story: she has been forced throughout her life to react to the demands of society. As a young and marriageable woman, she has never been able to act. Her movements have been defensive, aimed at protecting her image from any impurity, her life from any gossip. Lily's purpose in life is to react, to respond, to the social code that originates and reinforces established power. Lily herself, as a would-be actor, has no power.

Wharton sets up the first scene, Lily's going to Selden's apartment, to illustrate Lily's powerlessness, her very lack of any pretense toward action. We have seen that her story at that moment is co-opted by Selden: he tells her story. He speculates on what she is doing at the train station. Lily does not tell the reader; eventually, she tells Selden. Her story is already being told—and thereby shaped—by someone who has no authority to tell it.

In the position Wharton creates for her, Lily has no authority. Had she been able to act, she would have found a tearoom herself. Instead, she waits for a "rescue," and she uses that word to Selden, continuing, "And I don't know what to do with myself." Strangely prophetic of Lily's course for the rest of her non-story, this plaintive pose leads her to suggest that they go to Selden's flat. Lily has acted: she shows her defiance of proper forms; she is engaging, honest, querulous, complaining. Things are amiss in her life, and she is surprisingly willing for Selden to know that they are.

Selden, however, responds too glibly. He is not capable of accepting Lily as a person but rather sees her as a costly object, the woman playing her dependent role. When Lily tells him, in as direct a language as she can employ, "What I want is a friend who won't be afraid to say disagreeable [things] when I need them. Sometimes I have fancied you might be that friend," Selden replies as if she were a complete stereotype, "Isn't marriage your vocation? Isn't it what you're all brought up for?" (9). By shifting to a plural form, Selden further diminishes Lily's personal plight, another clue that Selden is not worth her attention. Lily has earlier discriminated between herself and other women in her social group, saying matter-of-factly, "the other women—my best friends—well, they use me or abuse me; but they don't care a straw what happens to me" (9).

One of the reasons Wharton has begun Lily's narrated story with this episode is that she is establishing the rapport between Lily and

Selden, with its already clear warning that Selden is not the "rescuer" Lily thinks he is. As he turns away the compliment she has paid him by being forthright, he shows his need to distance himself from unconventional—and possibly lovable—women. But another reason to begin *The House of Mirth* with this scene is to establish the dangers the unconventional woman faces whenever she chooses to act for herself. As Lily leaves Selden's flat, Wharton uses her omniscient narrative voice to point out: "On the landing she paused to look about her. There were a thousand chances to one against her meeting anybody, but one could never tell, and she always paid for her rare indiscretions by a violent reaction of prudence. There was no one in sight, however, but a char-woman who was scrubbing the stairs" (13). Wharton's irony is immediate. The char-woman soon blackmails Lily by selling her the love letters to Selden, assuming that Lily is their author. Questionable behavior means a quick loss of innocence. A few steps further on, Lily meets Simon Rosedale, to whom she lies, saying that she has been visiting her dressmaker. Putting herself in Rosedale's power will prove dangerous; as she tells herself angrily, "That stupid story about her dress-maker was bad enough—it would have been so simple to tell Rosedale that she had been taking tea with Selden! The mere statement of the fact would have rendered it innocuous" (15). Wharton shows the reader clearly that Lily's existence is one defensive maneuver after another.

Readers of traditional novels expect protagonists to be brave, decisive, accomplished. It is no wonder that the critical reaction to Lily Bart as protagonist has been one of impatience. Lily cannot decide whether or not to be decisive; she needs to cut loose from those uncaring friends and stop playing these depressing—and futile—social games; she must settle on a man and marry him. Readers insist that Lily "succeed" in her role. Yet Wharton's point through the novel is that Lily does not want that expected success. It is her very "failure" in the social game that makes Lily a hero.

Under the trappings of a straightforward novel of manners, voiced through what seems to be an omniscient third-person consciousness, Wharton has written the story of a singular woman character. Lily Bart, even though she appears at times to be a fashionable manikin, one of the elite and beautiful women whose destiny is alloted to them from birth, is neither so simple nor so simply fated. Lily Bart is a confused outsider, a woman who is in all respects marginal to the system. She has too little money, and too much honesty, integrity, and scruples, to marry the "right" man. She insists on finding a man she could love. But because she knows herself to be a person of exquisite sensibility, who thoroughly enjoys—indeed, demands—the things great wealth provides, she knows her husband has to come from the extremely wealthy. In short, Lily's choices are very limited. Her dilemma is that she is too honest to accept any suitor she does not love. Wharton tells the reader this very early, in the dialogue at Selden's flat. When Selden urges Lily to marry, since it seems she is fated to do so, her hurt rejoinder is, "You speak as if I ought to marry the first man who came along" (9).

Wharton has taken the so-called "marriage plot" as the scaffolding of *The House of Mirth,* and made an active and elaborate plot from the simple man-meets-woman-and-they-marry outline. (The assumption in the novel of marriage is that such a state is ideal for both parties, especially the woman, so all activity ceases once the couple is married.) She has ironically described marriage after marriage, couple after couple, with marital infidelity of both husband and wife, and very little evidence of pleasure among any of them—either in each other or in the family life they have created. Everything a marriage accomplishes seems best defined in terms of financial acquisition; people marry to improve their social or financial position, and beautiful men and women who have no fortunes marry into money in exchange for their own beauty. Lily Bart's situation is the latter: she is the most beautiful of society's ornaments (and Wharton's early title for the novel was "A Moment's Ornament"), and in order to stay within the society she desires, she must marry the money required.

Lily never thinks of herself except as part of this high-status couples culture. Reared to be a successful socialite, she has not questioned her eventual destination. Now, eleven years after her debut, trying to pretend she is younger than her twenty-nine years, she is beginning to face the quandary of what she will do if she doesn't marry well. In her view, she has no other choice. The dour image Wharton shows Lily projecting, when she is forced to be realistic about her status, confirms Lily's vision of herself as a passive victim of society: "Lily seemed to watch her own figure retreating down vistas of neutral-tinted dullness to a middle age like Grace Stepney's. When she had ceased to amuse Judy Trenor and her friends she would have to fall back on amusing Mrs. Peniston; whichever way she looked she saw only a future of servitude to the whims of others, never the possibility of asserting her own eager individuality" (100). This bleak view combines with an unusual moment of self-disgust: "She knew herself by heart too, and was sick of the old story" (99).

Wharton's depiction of Lily here is not critical of her protagonist. She carefully shows that every other woman in *The House of Mirth* is trapped in the same romantic thralldom. The poor women in Gerty's care are all hopeful of a great love; even the sensible Gerty yearns for romance (and dreams of her cousin, Lawrence Selden). It is no accident that Wharton draws Lily and Gerty together at the "simple country wedding" of Jack Stepney and Gwen Van Osburgh, "to which guests are convoyed in special trains" (87). While the two women's responses to the lush wedding gifts differ, their attitudes are similar in essential ways. After portraying Gerty and Lily with arms linked as if they are best girlhood friends, Wharton demolishes Lily's confident assertion that she will, somehow, be herself married within the year. The wedding celebration is the scene of three unexpected blows to Lily's confidence.

First, she learns that Percy Gryce—one of her own former marital possibilities—is engaged to the youngest Van Osburgh; in this case, one large fortune augments another. Then she is literally touched ("what right had he to touch her?") by Gus Trenor, who booms that he has been speculating for her. Lily prefers to pretend that such an unorthodox financial arrangement does not exist, and she has not yet admitted to herself the threat that her being indebted to Gus might create. Trenor then brings social-climbing Sim Rosedale to Lily for a special greeting, but she instead snubs him, and gives him the opening to create a wry scene in front of Selden. (This time Selden makes no move to rescue her.) As the chapter ends, Wharton has taken Lily from a perch of extreme self-satisfaction, in which she plans her own wedding (bridegroom yet unnamed), through the loss of one of the most eligible of mates (and perhaps Selden as well), to the threatening behavior of both Trenor and Rosedale. The scene earlier is filled with jibes at Gerty's boundless romanticism, yet the reader feels that Lily's attitudes have been every bit as unrealistic. And for Lily, the stakes of believing in the efficacy of romance are much higher.

Wharton's ironic treatment of the artificially staged "country wedding" makes clear how complex—emotionally, financially, socially—every marriage must be. Lily's naive optimism about her own role as marriage partner is echoed in another major scene a bit later in the novel. Just as Lily believes that marriage is her destiny, so she believes that a woman's beauty is aesthetic pleasure in its purest form. She agrees to help stage, and participate in, the Wellington Brys's evening of *tableaux vivants,* without realizing that the sexual element in the disclosure of women's bodies is the strongest motivation for the crowd who watches. "Deuced bold thing to show herself in that get-up; but gad, there isn't a break in the lines anywhere, and I suppose she wanted us to know it!" Ned Van Alstyne's cynical appreciation captures the real tone of the effect of Lily's display, though Selden this time does rescue her from the crowd of eager admirers. Wharton gives us insight into that actual reception by having the blunt Gus Trenor exclaim about Lily, "Damned bad taste, I call it" (138). The difference between the pure woman men marry and the beautiful woman they covet—or purchase—is, for Lily, sometimes blurred. At this stage of her life in the marriage mart, she could not risk errors of judgment.

Lily's concept of herself as marriageable woman centers on the romantic and avoids the sexual dimension, whereas Wharton's choice of scenes in *The House of Mirth* stresses the sexual as the dominant motivation. In the fabric of innuendo and gossip that comprise "conversation," Lily's reputation is a prominent theme. Wharton creates the primary tension in the novel by setting Lily's real story against Lily's story as told by her society. The story of Lily Bart becomes the story of a reputation: the essence of Lily—with all her beauty, wily intelligence, and honesty—becomes that story. And although the reader knows that the women characters gossip (Mrs. Peniston knows everything that happens in the society from which she stays so disdainfully remote), Wharton's emphasis falls on the tale telling of the male characters. Trenor tells Rosedale about his financing Lily; Rosedale tells Trenor about Lily's lying as she came from Selden's flat; Percy Gryce tells his mother that Lily gambles; Lord Hubert tells Selden about the Duchess.

The most damage to Lily's standing in society, however, is done not by words but through the appearances she makes in questionable circumstances. The Brys's tableau is one such instance. The next is her going at night to Trenor's house, thinking that Judy is there. Admittedly Gus has blatantly tricked Lily; but observers know only that Gus and Lily are alone in his house, and she is seen leaving late at night. Even though Selden has been ready to express his love and has set a time the following day to come to Lily for that purpose, when he sees her leaving the Trenor house he loses all faith in her and sails for Europe.

Wharton ends book 1 with Lily's bleak realization: "She understood now that he was never coming, that he had gone away because he was afraid that he might come" (179), that the "rescue" she had thought Selden capable of was not going to materialize. The ending of book 1 is shrouded in silence. Selden has not communicated with Lily at all; she reads of his departure in the newspaper. Lily, then, has no recourse in language. She writes a letter to Selden, but has no way to reach him; she attempts to write to Rosedale, who has proposed marriage, but finally cannot bring herself to accept. The Brys's tableaux have informed the novel with a spirit of pantomime. The last image Wharton gives the reader is that of the beautiful Lily sitting "with her elbows on the table and her face hidden in her hands" (179).

By ending book 1 with Lily's intense pain over her abandonment, Wharton emphasizes the force of money in her protagonist's life. Lily's involvement with Gus Trenor occurs because she needs funds. When Gus threatens her, it is always in financial terms: he wants some value for his investment. Her openness to Sim Rosedale—her even considering his proposal—results from his approaching her as though marriage were a business proposition. She understands Rosedale's intent, and finds his honesty more appealing than Gus's subterfuge. Mrs. Peniston's displeasure with Lily is over the scandal she has created in being linked with Trenor, as much as it is over the large amount of money she has spent. Ironically, if Lily had had family money, she would not have gotten involved in Trenor's investment plan—and the scandal would not have occurred. Wharton's insistence that readers pay attention to the economic details of Lily's plight is reflected in Lily's family name (*Bart*, possibly suggestive of the word *barter*, the medium of exchange for people without currency) and in the title of the book itself. *The House of Mirth* suggests a mercantile establishment more directly than it echoes the Ecclesiastes verse that Wharton intended to use as an epigraph to the book but later removed: "The heart of fools is in the house of mirth."

Lily's propensity to maintain a romantic view, to discount her debts, and to think she will eventually be rescued somehow, makes her the prototype of the innocent American girl (if not the foolish virgin). But in Wharton's fictional country, innocence is no excuse; romance is only the stuff of fairy tales and does not belong in Lily's increasingly sad story.

six

The Structure

By dividing *The House of Mirth* into two sections, each written in a different pace, Wharton forces the reader's attention to the pivotal point that centers the novel. Book 1 ends with Lily's despair after she realizes that Selden has, literally, fled from her. As a man of words, Selden's failure to use language either to ascertain or to explain what he thinks is her indiscretion in Trenor's house is heavily ironic. Selden's "love" has no grounding in any reality and, like most sham structures of belief, cannot stand any testing. Again, Wharton plays on the reader's understanding of romance. She draws a narrowly conventional attitude for Selden, who insists that Lily be the pure virginal maiden if she is to win his love. Wharton's irony, which undercuts Selden's disillusion, shows itself in her description of the scene between Lily and Trenor, the scene that sends Selden out of the country so swiftly: "two figures were seen silhouetted against the hall-light. At the same moment a hansom halted at the curbstone, and one of the figures floated down to it in a haze of evening draperies; while the other, black and bulky, remained persistently projected against the light" (160–61). Wharton's vague indefiniteness here leads the reader to question Selden's response. Positive identification of the silhouettes is unlikely; any graceful woman would "float" to the cab. The wry description of the male figure takes on a tinge of Selden's perspective. Trenor, about whom Selden has already felt great repugnance, thinking of his "fat creased hands" (154), deserves no fonder description than "black and bulky"—and persistent.

Selden's running away from knowledge about Lily's behavior is especially ironic because Selden has praised his own difference from other men in that he is philosophically open-minded. He has insisted that Lily have freedom, that she explore her circumstances rather than simply accept what society mandates. If any man should be willing at least to talk with her about the Trenor house episode, Selden should. Yet Wharton ends book 1 here, adding the emphasis of a major narrative break to the surprise the reader feels at Selden's unexpected behavior.

The first half of *The House of Mirth* has privileged Selden's view of both Lily and the world. Much of the narrative has been seen through Selden's eyes, and recounted through his voice. The reader assumes his credibility and is ready to step into the familiar role of relying on a male narrator, even if that narrator is far removed from the protagonist. As Judith Fetterley has said so well, "recognition and reiteration, not difference and expansion, provide the motivation for reading." Readers want confirmation of expected patterns, and if the male character is not the protagonist, he might well be the narrator, the guide to understanding the story. Fetterley continues, "reading functions primarily to reinforce the identity and perspective which the male teacher/reader brings to the text. Presumably this function is itself a function of the sense of power derived from the experience of perceiving one's self as central, as subject, . . . because [one is] literally the point of view from which the rest of the world is seen. Thus men, controlling the study of literature, define as great those texts that empower themselves."[17] Wharton has given the reader this expected paradigm, a male narrator and observer, to allow the reader to make sense of the partially hidden motivations of the female protagonist. But with the beginning of book 2, that structure changes. Wharton's narrative method thus supports the complexity of her novel's theme: *The House of Mirth* is not about the typical young woman headed for a good marriage; it is about the maverick young woman who resists the social code that would coerce her into wifehood.

The skill with which Wharton draws Lily has sometimes gone unnoticed. Lily's hesitancy, her almost vacuous acceptance of what Selden tells her, is at the heart of her reality—and Wharton has prepared the reader for that reality in the early description of her, standing "apart from the crowd, letting it drift by her." Lily Bart is *not* complicit in this society's expectations for women; she is herself an observer. Through her choice of narrative method, Wharton forces the reader into asking several key questions. How could Lily Bart, reared by the most self-serving of mothers to think that her only worth was in her beauty, surrounded by a society that plays the marriage game even more ruthlessly than it plays bridge (and for higher stakes), sent into the world with neither formal education nor means of learning other ways to challenge those that prevail; how could this strangely sheltered woman know where to begin to learn about alternate ways of living and choices? Selden's is the only voice that seems to have a wider perspective, that seems to be encouraging her to think differently than do her friends and relatives.

Whenever Lily follows his lead, however, she ends up with new problems, difficulties that would not have been hers if she had stayed on the expected social track. Selden derides her marrying for money, yet when she loses Percy Gryce, Selden has no alternative. He challenges her to think more philosophically even if doing so will put her at odds with her society. He approves of her showing her artistic ability—and her beauty—in the very tableau that makes her the target of envy and gossip among her friends. By not marrying, however, Lily is more and more dependent on other people's money, more easily at the mercy of Trenor, Rosedale, and their kind. And when Selden might have spoken his love and given Lily—the reader supposes—some ideal marriage, he runs out with no explanation and, more importantly, no opportunity for her to discuss the situation. Selden's actions announce that Lily is beneath his notice or support. She is blamed and judged with no defense or appeal; and, as book 2 shows, she is rapidly found guilty.

The key to Lily's character lies in the very insubstantiality of personality Wharton draws so carefully in book 1. Despite her age, Lily is a child, and *The House of Mirth* is in some ways a bildungsroman: Lily's story is that of her education. Unfortunately, she has as her school only the society in which she lives, and the mistakes she makes as she tests the system are irreparable. The social group that would protect her were she to behave as she is expected to behave will not aid her when her behavior threatens their social code. Judy Trenor loves the Lily who will play secretary and cosset her cross husband in exchange for hospitality, but she abandons her when she seems to be on too-familiar terms with that husband. A useful Lily is one who serves the system; a defiant, questioning, or uncontrollable Lily is dangerous. Lily's description of Bertha Dorset's relative power (in that Bertha has a house and an opera box, whereas Lily is poor) is as naive as Lily herself at the start of the novel. Bertha has power because Bertha represents the system, and whatever she does, her behavior is sanctioned by that system. To challenge Bertha is to challenge the structure and consequently everyone within it.

The early liaison between Selden and the married Bertha is further testimony to Selden's unreliability as narrator. Rather than separate himself from the system, Selden lives off it. Under cover of Bertha's strong social position, their affair has been known but allowed. The affair is over. The letters Lily buys from Mrs. Haffen, in order to "protect" her society and particularly Selden, seem to be entreaties from Bertha, and her behavior when Lily chooses to be with Selden instead of Percy Gryce indicates that she regards Selden as her property still. What Wharton emphasizes in book 2—the flagrant liaison between Bertha and Ned Silverton and its scandalous denouement, which Bertha manipulates to discredit Lily—is a suggestive replaying of what might have been the relationship between Bertha and Selden. Imagined in the role Neddy Silverton plays during book 2, Selden can have little pretense to moral superiority.

The Lily Bart Wharton draws in book 1 is vacillating, thrown off balance by Selden's glowing rhetoric so that she questions the premises that have always guided her. Critical of the society she yet longs to stay a part of, she is hardly the resolute traditional hero. But, given her uncertain position in her social world, given the imperative to play ingenue until she marries, the most promising traits Lily has are her tentativeness and her willingness to question. Frances Restuccia sees the real duality between Selden and Lily as being Selden's need for fixity, a stable understanding of social roles and codes, set against Lily's mutability. Lily will wait and see what she should do, think, become; Selden has to have his proper role established consistently. Describing what she calls "Lily's book-long oscillation," Restuccia notes: "While Lily refuses positions of stability, Selden, faithful to his profession, locates them where they are nonexistent. Selden must transform ambiguity to clarity, as he does in his reading of Lily's story. We might expect, consequently, that, given the instability—the constitutive ambiguity—of language, Selden would shy away from writing."[18] Seeing Lily's wavering uncertainty as positive and strong, this critic only supports the reading that Selden is an untrustworthy narrator, and that Wharton's use of his observations is another facet of her deeply entrenched irony.

Between books 1 and 2, Wharton allows Lily Bart to disappear. Much of what the reader would like to know about Lily after Selden's leave-taking—when it is evident that Lily is shaken and confused by Trenor's duplicity—is unstated. Wharton builds to the ending of the first book by showing the reader Lily's long wait for Selden's appearance at tea, her discovery of his departure in the newspaper, and her own invitation to go abroad with Bertha Dorset.

Book 1 stops abruptly, and book 2 begins just as abruptly. The reader is left to imagine the intervening three months. As in the first half of the novel, at the start of the second book Wharton focuses on Lawrence Selden. Several months after his rush away from Lily, Selden has spent the winter working hard at the law and has only recently come abroad again, this time in connection with his work. The irony of Wharton's training the reader's attention on Selden, when Lily is the strong center of interest, establishes the premise for the rest of book 2. Society remains in control, and Selden—as sophisticated intellectual, an integral part of that society—remains an important voice in the narration. The narrative, once again, comes to the reader through his point of view.

The opening of book 2 is reminiscent of the opening of the novel: Selden is observing society in Monte Carlo. Here Wharton describes his life as a "spectatorship," and his quest as the search for order. Her phrase "his fixed sky" reminds the reader of his frustration early in the novel because he could not "fix" Lily and her movements into the patterns he anticipated. The beauty of the Monte Carlo twilight, in fact, reminds Selden of the last moments of some panoramic "tableau" (183–84). Wharton has deliberately connected the Selden in book 2 with the Selden the reader knew throughout book 1.

After this introduction and stage setting, Wharton focuses Selden's attention (as spectator) on "a consciously conspicuous group of people [obviously Americans]," and soon the reader hears news of Lily Bart. Immediately the action begins, with Lily described as imprudent, or flighty, or something more quixotic. In the words of the astute survivor, Carry Fisher: "That's Lily all over, you know: she works like a slave preparing the ground and sowing her seed; but the day she ought to be reaping the harvest she oversleeps herself or goes off on a picnic. . . . Sometimes I think it's because, at heart, she despises the things she's trying for" (189).

Book 2 is a series of climactic and defeating episodes for Lily. In almost every instance, Selden observes; he often helps her make an escape, but the fact is that Lily is on the run, pursued by the machinations of Bertha Dorset—and the reader cannot forget that Bertha's initial anger with Lily occurred over Selden. The irony of his adopting the role of Lily's "rescuer" in light of his also being part of the cause of Bertha's pursuit is inescapable.

Lily's problems are exacerbated by her poverty. Wharton structures *The House of Mirth* so that immediately after Bertha has ordered Lily off the *Sabrina,* the novel moves with cinematic quickness to the reading of Mrs. Peniston's will. Changed after news of Lily's supposed liaison with George Dorset has reached Mrs. Peniston, the will leaves Lily only ten thousand dollars, in effect disinheriting her.

The visible decline in Lily's fortunes, both financial and emotional, is drawn in Wharton's clipped, fast-paced narrative: the pace of the story distances the reader from Lily's futile attempts to recover. There is to be no recovery, however, even when Rosedale urges Lily to go to Bertha with the letters and demand apology and restitution in society.

Wharton's reliance on the packet of Bertha's letters—and her mention of it throughout the book—reminds the reader of the duplicitous social system, and of Lily's innocence in contrast to that system. Just as Mrs. Haffen mistakes Lily for the author of the letters, so society judges

THE HOUSE OF MIRTH

her falsely. Yet Lily's goodness—which prompts her to purchase the letters in the first place—prevents her using them, either with Bertha or with Selden. When she throws the shadowy packet into Selden's fire after yet another inconsequential and indirect interchange, the reader feels that the letters symbolize Lily's last hope. Selden's utter inability either to see or to hear what Lily has come to is one of the more poignant scenes in the novel. Lily goes on talking, insistently, and the narrative voice describes the urgency the reader feels: "Whether he wished it or not, he must see her wholly for once before they parted" (307).

After their conversation, Lily tells Selden good-bye in several ways, throwing the letters into the fire. Whatever good the letters might have been in some previous life, they have no efficacy in Lily's present bleak world. They seem, to her, completely unreal.

Wharton concludes the scene with the letters burned, with no use ever to be made of their words, their presence. Just as Selden did not care about those words—for Mrs. Haffen had found the letters in his waste basket—so he does not know how to care for Lily's words. He literally cannot understand them, nor can he reply to them. Wharton ends the scene with the image of Selden, "tranced . . . still groping for the word to break the spell" (310). Reminiscent of the language of fairy tales, Selden's "spell" is a selfish luxury. Lily, still cold and wet from being caught in the rain, kisses him goodbye and walks back to her solitary room. Her kiss has not awakened him, any more than has her language.

Following Wharton's clues, the reader knows now that there will be no rescue by Selden, for Selden himself has been cast in the role of love object, in need of both awakening and rescue.

Lily's kiss may have had a long-term effect, for the ironic opening of Wharton's last chapter shows an ebullient Selden hurrying toward Lily's flat at only nine in the morning. Clearly now awakened from his trance-like state, Selden is both ready to act and armed with the word which has previously eluded him. Wharton has called the reader's attention to the metaphor of exchanging words when she has, just a page earlier, shown Lily's inability to find a word for which she groped, "some word she had found that should make life clear between them" (323), going into the drugged sleep that would mean her death. In this "mild and bright" morning scene, part of Selden's "youthful sense of adventure" shows itself in his confidence—in both language and self. He is, clearly and ironically, completely in charge: "Nine o'clock was an early hour for a visit, but Selden had passed beyond all such conventional observances. He only knew that he must see Lily Bart at once—he had found the word he meant to say to her, and it could not wait another moment to be said. It was strange that it had not come to his lips sooner—that he had let her pass from him the evening before without being able to speak it. But what did that matter, now that a new day had come? (324)." Wharton's rhetorical question, "But what did that matter," punctures the mood of both Selden and reader. For time has mattered, and Selden's complete insensitivity to Lily's physical and mental state has kept him from responding as he might have, and when he might have.

Wharton continues her reversal of expected imagery by stressing the brilliance of Lily's death bed: "The irresistible sunlight poured a tempered golden flood into the room, and in its light Selden saw a narrow bed along the wall, and on the bed, with motionless hands and calm unrecognizing face, the semblance of Lily Bart" (325). The narrow, and chaste, bed symbolizes Lily's life—pure, inviolate, crowded next to a wall in a modest room, never to escape from sterile loneliness into the warmth of care and wealth.

When Wharton describes Lily's figure as a "semblance," the reader is alerted to the fictionality of Selden's observations. As at the beginning of the novel, the reader is in the power of Selden as narrator: the account of Lily's denouement will come from his eyes, and Lily dead is even more the object that Selden had described her as being in chapter 1.

It is significant that Wharton never lets Selden touch Lily. He thinks of laying his face along hers, he considers some passion in a leave-taking, but his legalistic mind interrupts and warns that time is short. So Selden—hardly destroyed by his passion—begins his scrutiny of Lily's effects, and nearly judges wrong when he comes to the financial matters. His shallow comprehension, his inaccurate guesses, are nowhere more obviously exposed than in Lily's room, and Wharton's care to make the reader see Selden's bumbling only intensifies Lily's separateness. If the man who could have married her, the man she would have loved, is only this inept interpreter, then Lily's life of loneliness might not have changed so much in marriage as she would have wished.

Wharton's last four paragraphs serve as an ironic coda, an authorial statement about Selden's vapidity so cleverly phrased, in what might have been his own words, that the reader wonders at the range of possible interpretations. Read literally, the section adds to Selden's self-congratulation: he has loved Lily, he claims, and he is somehow helping her at that moment. He would be comforted in his nostalgia; he would have the memory of their love, even if he had never spoken of it to her. "But at least he *had* loved her—had been willing to stake his future on his faith in her—and if the moment had been fated to pass from them before they could seize it, he saw now that, for both, it had been saved whole out of the ruin of their lives" (329).

More than ironic, Selden's statement is also vapid and meaningless. How could the moment be saved for *both* when Lily is already dead? Selden's obeisance to "fate," the rationalization that what had happened to Lily was bound to happen, is even further mockery of her belief in him. Wharton's setting Selden in the position of Lily's rescuer now appears to have been a device of biting censure, as the reader sees that the central trait of Selden's personality is his unwillingness to take any stand that calls for action. And his meaningless phrase, "the ruin of their lives," is another empty nod to the sentimental novel. While Lily is unquestionably dead, Selden's life is hardly a "ruin." It might be said to be flourishing, in fact. Selden has escaped not only marriage to Lily, but also any involvement in her unfairly maligned life—and with her burning of Bertha's letters, Selden has also escaped any later ramifications of that affair.

Selden's definition of "love" in this passage is also self-serving. Staking his future on his faith in her does not represent Selden's behavior as Wharton has described it throughout the book. Where was Selden's faith when Lily left the Trenor house at midnight? Where was his support during the long two years when she fell so thoroughly out of place, and out of sight, of the society to which he also belongs? What Selden's words in this concluding chapter show, forcefully, is that he will use all events to aggrandise himself. Even though he could rightly be contrite, could blame himself for being the last person to see Lily alive and the last who had some chance of saving her, he never admits to any complicity. He instead ennobles his part in the travesty of Lily's decline by creating a fiction about what he and Lily have shared. In Selden's rhetoric, they shared this great love; they shared this moment; and, finally, they shared "the word which made all clear" (329).

In this chapter, Wharton uses Selden's words against him. First, he claims to know the word, and then he claims to share that word with Lily—as if any understanding about a subject as complex as love could be captured in a single word, even if the dead woman were able to hear it. If the legalistic Selden doesn't realize the quixotic evanescence of words, Wharton does. And so do Wharton's readers, who have just read a novel of thousands of words and now find that they have no idea what word Selden refers to. The riddlelike effect of the ending—Selden's calling attention to a word that he does not name, and the reader cannot guess— adds to the reader's dismay. Here at the end of Lily's story, Selden not only is shown as seriously limited in his use of language, he also appears as a self-serving egoist. As Dale M. Bauer points out: "Lily is the text that remains incomprehensible for Selden; he is no critic, no identificatory reader, able to transform the text or himself from confronting alien thoughts and allowing the division to occur between the subject formed by his culture and his experience of the effects of that ideology in Lily's death ... because the finalizing word is left unsaid, the novel remains open-ended. Lily does not deliver a final word about herself; her suicide serves, instead, as a means to stave off others' essentializing discourse about her."[19]

Perhaps Wharton's fullest irony is that even Lily's death does not leave Selden at any loss for words. Selden not only "explains" and justifies throughout the scene in Lily's death room; he also convinces himself by the end of his time there that he and Lily have had a monumental love affair, and that her death has kept their love pure, safe from the tawdry dailiness of actual living relationships. It is Selden's self-praise that makes the concluding chapter so revelatory, and turns him from a character who bores and frustrates the reader into one who disturbs. For if the narrative of women's lives falls into hands such as these, to be told through a voice such as this and in such inaccurate language as this, readers have no chance of ever learning the significance of women's stories.

Wharton's choosing to write this concluding section so as to bring the reader into an intimate relation with Selden—in all his vacuous and offensive hypocrisy—does several important things. First, it conveys an indisputable argument for Lily's naiveté. The very man she thought was so superior to her, the man to whom she looked for guidance and encouragement, was incapable of recognizing her very substantial strengths. Selden never saw Lily at all *as she was*. He saw her first as the manacled victim of the society that had made her, and he saw her, dead, as the woman he had loved tragically, whose love he had been fated to lose.

Second, the novel's ending acknowledges the complicity of Lily's society—*all* her society—in her death. If Selden is presented as somehow superior to the herd, then his superiority is itself egregiously flawed. As Wharton said to Sara Norton, Selden is a "negative hero," and her publisher's urging that her next novel have stronger men because he was tired of critical comments about Selden reinforced the sense that many readers of *The House of Mirth* found that character irritating.[20]

Perhaps most important, at least to readers contemporary with the novel's publication in 1905, the conclusion allows *The House of Mirth* a traditional "marriage novel" structure. If the expected ending was the marriage of the protagonists, then the scene of the lamenting Selden, kneeling near Lily's dead body, is a satisfactory denouement— the marriage novel frustrated. A lover's sorrow is as acceptable as a lover's happiness, especially when the bereaved can make such poetic and heartfelt use of his loss. With Lily's death, many readers critical of her sometimes unpredictable behavior are satisfied; because she has disappeared from the story, the reader need make no judgment about her behavior or her life. And because her death has been "accidental," the reader has nowhere to place any blame. The reader can join with Selden in the self-congratulation of their sensitive response to Lily's tragic—and unnecessary—death.

As Wharton knew well, however, a great many of her readers would not accept that final chapter as a traditional ending and would see it as the subtle unmasking of the still inaccurate narrator, Lawrence Selden.

seven
_____

The Mother-Daughter Paradigm

Although *The House of Mirth* ends with a chapter told from Selden's point of view, with Lily an artifact of sentimentality rather than a real, dead woman, Lily's story more appropriately ends in the chapter before this. The last glimpse readers have of Lily alive is her waking from a drugged sleep to imagine that she has lost the child she has been holding, a fantasy she had experienced as she fell asleep. Wharton describes Lily's feeling of interruption in the drowsy peace the chloral had induced: "through which, of a sudden, a dark flush of loneliness and terror tore its way. She started up again, cold and trembling with the shock: for a moment she seemed to have lost her hold of the child. But no—she was mistaken—the tender pressure of its body was still close to hers" (323).

Wharton juxtaposes this agony of loneliness and terror, the mood most obvious in Lily's rootless life, with the reassurance of the baby's warmth. Yet within the many narrative paths of the novel, until the last few chapters, there has been no mention of Lily's desire to be a mother or of her interest in children; the reader has seen no children at all within the fashionable Trenor-Dorset society. Wharton introduces the real baby through the person of Nettie Struther, the woman Lily's gift to Gerty's charity has helped, a woman who has learned to love again after being seduced and abandoned by her first lover. "Marry Anto'nette," as she has named her daughter, is the product of Nettie's marriage to the loving man who "knew about" her but still wanted to marry her, and Wharton's misspelling and misidentification of the child intensifies the reader's recognition of the ironic reversals of Nettie's and Lily's roles. The still virginal Lily, a member of the "protected" class, is ruined because her society assumes she has grown sexually experienced. Her value in the marriage mart has fallen to nothing; she has been abandoned by everyone who has power, even by Selden, the supposedly liberal man who has intimated that he loves her. She probably will never marry and have children. Yet Nettie, who as a working girl had no protection and was sexually victimized, has found a loving and forgiving husband, and her infant daughter is the result of that union.

As Lily sits in the warmth of Nettie's small kitchen, watching her feed the baby, she realizes everything she has missed. The women's wordless understanding prompts Lily to ask to hold the child, and that trusting weight in her arms "thrilled her with a sense of warmth and returning life." As Lily leaves the Struther flat, she feels her deep depression lift under "the surprised sense of human fellowship." Wharton says pointedly in this scene that Lily feels "as though the child entered into her and became a part of herself" (316).

The remaining sections that Wharton adds to follow the Struther scene complete the image of Lily Bart at thirty-one, and give added poignance to her return to "human fellowship." Once she comes back to her room, Lily retraces her recent life by spreading her few remaining gowns—"survivals of her last phase of splendour, on the *Sabrina* and in London"—on her bed, realizing that the memories the sight of them evoked *were* her life. Their very lack of substance and warmth, in contrast to the physical presence of the child, contributes to Lily's growing resignation.

The delivery of her ten thousand dollar bequest from Mrs. Peniston's estate provides Lily's second, and last, activity. She pays all her bills, including the check of repayment to Gus Trenor, and then Wharton whirls her back into the nostalgia for belonging and rootedness that her glimpse of real life and family has evoked. The imagery Wharton chooses to describe Lily's mood leaves no mystery about the real causes of her depression:

> there was something more miserable still—it was the clutch of solitude at her heart, the sense of being swept like a stray uprooted growth down the heedless current of the years. That was the feeling which possessed her now—the feeling of being something rootless and ephemeral, mere spindrift of the whirling surface of existence, without anything to which the poor little tentacles of self could cling before the awful flood submerged them. And as she looked back she saw that there had never been a time when she had had any real relation to life. Her parents too had been rootless, blown hither and thither on every wind of fashion, without any personal existence to shelter them from its shifting gusts. (319)

One of the tragedies of Lily's life, as Wharton has insisted throughout the novel, is that she had no home, no caring family, particularly no mother, to guide and support her: the theme of mother-daughter relationship is imaged in Nettie's female child. When Wharton emphasizes the effect on Lily of the natural yet miraculous scene, its echoing through Lily's distraught consciousness is entirely plausible. Rather than remember the dissatisfaction she found at Selden's (despite the fact that she had given him every opportunity to understand her situation and her feelings, and had burned the letters that might have paid her way back into society), Lily's lingering memory is of the love and warmth Nettie's household offered to her. And the physical touch of the child's body would be an integral part of that memory, contrasted emphatically with the lack of touch between Lily and Selden.

Lily's sleeping in the fantasy of holding a child is also plausible if it is seen as Lily's retreat to a childlike stage, admitting her need to be cared for. Her absent mother—the mother who never had Lily's interests at heart but viewed her beautiful daughter as a means to wealth and position—has been a much more important psychological factor in her life than some readings of *The House of Mirth* suggest. Wharton's strategy early in the book is to describe Lily as a child and to show the reader the terse, and tense, relationship between Mr. and Mrs. Bart, the struggle for money dominating their pairing and their existence. On the first night, Wharton shows the reader Lily's disturbed sleep after she has played bridge at Bellomont and lost a great deal of money; she remembers her mother's saying "with a kind of fierce vindictiveness: 'But you'll get it all back—you'll get it all back, with your face'" (28). Her thoughts continue on a train of related ideas, and the reader surmises that these memories are as upsetting as Lily's evening—and financial loss—has been.

In her first conversation with Selden, Lily mentions her lack of family and her dependence on her aunt, who cares very little what becomes of her (provided that she does not disgrace the family name in some way). Wharton is clearly developing the theme that Lily is an unprotected woman who has no sustenance from her remaining family, just as she seems to have had none from her parents. Lily's childhood was spent, Wharton points out, in "the turbulent element called home," a place ruled by "the vigorous and determined figure" of her mother. The Barts' marriage seeming to be a power struggle, Lily grew up in New York— plotting to go abroad for treasures of dress and society—and in Europe, plundering that territory for the booty of a place in society.

Lily remembers her childhood home as "a house in which no one dined at home unless there was 'company'; a door-bell perpetually ringing; a hall-table showered with square envelopes which were opened in haste, and oblong envelopes which were allowed to gather dust . . . quarrels in the pantry, the kitchen and the drawing-room" (28–29). It is during the comparative intimacy of a Saturday lunch that Mr. Bart's financial failure is revealed. After Lily entreats her father for permission to buy six-dozen lillies-of-the-valley each day, to use as luncheon table flowers, he laughs ironically and announces that he is ruined, a word repeated three times in the ensuing conversation. Then Wharton writes a remarkable single paragraph, telescoping events in Mr. Bart's life so that, at the paragraph's end, he dies.

Wharton seemed content with a facade of Bart as breadwinner (and an unsatisfactory breadwinner at that, from Mrs. Bart's perspective). Her intentionally flat characterization serves an important narrative purpose: the reader is seeing Bart only through the eyes of his critical wife, just as, throughout the novel, the reader sees Lily only through the observing eyes of her critical society. And just as Lily, dead, is viewed through another character's perspective, so is her father: "To his wife he no longer counted: he had become extinct when he ceased to fulfil his purpose, and she sat at his side with the provisional air of a traveller who waits for a belated train to start" (33). It is likely intentional that Wharton creates the same kind of fate for Lily, also "ruined" in the eyes of her culture. She shortly takes to her bed to die as well. Trapped in a rigid society whose imperative was that people "win," men who could not succeed monetarily, and women who could not succeed socially, met the same relentless fate.

Lily's mother is shown to be uninterested in Lily, except as a commodity to buoy the family through its financial misfortunes. When she dies of disappointment and the loss of her hard-won social position, Lily is left with very little. Though her father's sister, Julia Peniston, takes Lily in because "no one else would have her," Mrs. Peniston— whose name suggests both *penance* and *stone*—feels no sympathy for her niece. Wharton describes the aunt clearly: "she had the kind of moral *mauvaise honte* which makes the public display of selfishness difficult, though it does not interfere with its private indulgence." Her initial grudging agreement—"I'll try her for a year"—suggests her lack of enthusiasm (36).

On several occasions, Wharton details Mrs. Peniston's character so that the reader understands that Lily's future is in obvious peril. Her aunt's veneration of "appearances" means that Lily's lack of attention to social forms will affront her aunt as well as her peers. The character of the parasitic Grace Stepney is another means of insuring Lily's downfall, for Grace conveys all gossip about Lily directly to her aunt.

Wharton uses dramatic irony in several of the scenes between Mrs. Peniston and Lily. The reader understands how vindictive Julia Peniston will be should Lily misbehave. Lily, unfortunately, has come to believe that she is safe within her "family," and that all she needs to do is confess to Aunt Julia and her financial problems will be resolved. Lily has accepted the notion of family responsibility, and relies on its existence.

Just as Lily cannot believe that her aunt will not help her repay her debts, so she cannot believe that her friends no longer *are* her friends. Being ignored by people who once cared for her leaves Lily incredulous. The greatest horror she can imagine, as she says to Gerty after her aunt's will has been read, is that people are "going to cut" her (225). It is Lily's tendency to believe that people are basically good; such an assumption leads her from one error of judgment to another, and finds her trusting Bertha Dorset enough to take the *Sabrina* cruise which ends so disastrously for Lily's reputation.

Lily's lament that she did, in fact, need a mother like Mrs. Van Osburgh, a woman who was able to place "four dull and dumpy daughters . . . in enviable niches of existence," points to an obvious truth. As circuitous as the ritual of courtship and marriage in Lily's society was, an inexperienced girl—on her own—had little chance of arranging all parts of that ritual for success. As Lily says enviously about the Van Osburghs, "Ah, lucky girls who grow up in the shelter of a mother's love—a mother who knows how to contrive opportunities without conceding favours, how to take advantage of propinquity without allowing appetite to be dulled by habit!" (91). The reader has no reason to doubt the honesty of Lily's statement.

Viewed from the perspective of her being a girl in need of mothering, Wharton's sometimes baffling protagonist is more nearly explicable. Childlike, Lily follows a path of action based on her trust that people are helpful and kind. Because she has always been a beauty, Lily is accustomed to finding herself the center of both attention and envy. She is quick to accept the former, and much too ready to discount the latter. She accordingly leaves herself open to attack.

At many places in *The House of Mirth*, Lily needs the "shelter" she had described in connection with a mother's love. By focusing the reader's attention on the image of *house* in the title, Wharton establishes the pervasive icon of a protective shelter that is linked with the word *mirth*. For all its positive tone, however, Wharton's "house of mirth" is not equated with the even more positive word *home*. Wharton underlines the intentional separation of *house* from *home* by using the noun *house* in Lily's early memory of the structure that was her home: "a house in which no one dined at home . . . a door-bell perpetually ringing." A noisy house such as Lily remembers does not make a home, and her lament about being "rootless and ephemeral" continues past the image of her parents' rootlessness to this segment:

> She herself had grown up without any one spot of earth being dearer to her than another: there was no centre of early pieties, of grave endearing traditions, to which her heart could revert and from which it could draw strength for itself and tenderness for others. In whatever form a slowly-accumulated past lives in the blood—whether in the concrete image of the old house stored with visual memories, or in the conception of the house not built with hands, but made up of inherited passions and loyalties—it has the same power of broadening and deepening the individual existence, of attaching it by mysterious links of kinship to all the mighty sum of human striving. (319)

When Lily is in need of this sheltering, she has only one place to go: to Gerty Farish. A surrogate mother figure (in that she is too dowdy to be a rival, and her obvious admiration for Lily gives her stability in one respect), Gerty is a constant friend and helpmeet. The most important scene in this pattern of Lily's reliance on Gerty and the shelter she can provide is her coming to Gerty's flat after she literally runs away from the Trenor house at midnight. As they lie in bed together, Gerty stays away from Lily, knowing that her friend usually does not want to be touched in any way. On this occasion, however, Lily begins sobbing and in her anguish, gropes for Gerty's hand "and held it fast.

> "Hold me, Gerty, hold me, or I shall think of things," she moaned; and Gerty silently slipped an arm under her, pillowing her head in its hollow as a mother makes a nest for a tossing child. In the warm hollow Lily lay still and her breathing grew low and regular. Her hand still clung to Gerty's as if to ward off evil dreams. (167)

Wharton's clear description of Lily as child here foreshadows Lily's fantasy of holding the sleeping child as she enters her last night of rest. The images of warmth, touch, and protection help the reader to align Lily's distraught state with a much more infantile and primary state of restlessness. The intentional symmetry that results from Wharton's manipulation of these scenes—one at the center, the other at the end of Lily's story—forces the reader to see how central to Lily's character, and outcome, has been the lack of family support and integrity.

Just as there is little mirth within Wharton's ironically titled house, so there is as little semblance of family. And throughout the whole course of Lily's life, there is only a vestige of anything bearing a resemblance to a mother.

eight

Story as Subtext

Contemporary literary critics are much more aware than their predecessors of the problems of women and minority writers who express themselves in work that must find both publishers and readers. When the themes and views of the writers are not those of the mainstream culture, the risk of offending that culture is great—and for a writer who has to live by his or her work, offending publishers and book buyers is not a profitable tactic.

Sandra M. Gilbert and Susan Gubar, in their important *The Madwoman in the Attic: The Woman Writer and the Nineteenth-Century Literary Imagination,* discuss what they term the "anxiety of authorship" felt by women writers who were excluded by class and profession from the ranks of mainstream authors—and the resulting subterfuge those writers had to employ in order for their work to be published.[21] More recently, Rachel Blau DuPlessis has surveyed a great amount of twentieth century writing, both fiction and poetry, and concludes that many women writers created tactics that enabled them to write books that the established literary market could appreciate and enjoy, while yet subtly criticizing—even ridiculing—the very principles these writers seemed to be following. DuPlessis contends in *Writing*

Beyond the Ending: Narrative Strategies of Twentieth-Century Women Writers that "to change story signals a dissent from social norms as well as narrative forms."[22] Wharton's *The House of Mirth* epitomizes this linked perspective, and as countless readers since the novel's publication in 1905 have commented, the author is criticizing much about the common practices of upper-class society. What differs between the reading of a 1980s person and that of a reader seventy years earlier is the assessment of what those practices and conventions really are.

Wharton criticized New York society by making Lily Bart its victim, and by showing that, regardless of what Lily had done, her end would have been unsatisfactory. No reader would be pleased had Lily married Percy Gryce, Sim Rosedale, or—after he admitted what Bertha was capable of—George Dorset. *The House of Mirth,* then, was never intended to be a domestic novel or a marriage novel—a story of manners that would reflect the times and end (no doubt) happily in a heterosexual marriage. It was not meant to be the instructive novel of morals, the message of which would probably confirm the established values of mainstream society. It was meant, rather, to be an ironic statement about such fictions, written when Wharton was well past the age of caring whether or not she had made a "good" marriage, having admitted to herself what an empty ritual marriage itself could be.[23]

Readers who look for ways to change Lily, to make her learn from her years as a marriageable woman, will be disappointed. Wharton's only answer is that the social system is so flawed that even the most innocent woman cannot escape being victimized—unless she comes endowed with financial power of her own, as do the Van Osburgh daughters. Wharton's initial scene of Lily's waiting between trains, fastidiously careful not to get hot or dirty, at the mercy not only of train schedules but of male interpretations of her acts and life, is a resonating image throughout the novel. When the reader first sees her, she is caught, trapped by events not of her own determination. One might say that of her as she takes the overdose of chloral in her small, grim room.

With a tone and themes radically different from those of most turn-of-the-century marriage novels, *The House of Mirth* adds complication to complication, irony to irony, until the reader can anticipate nothing more. The sense of careful unwinding that leads to Lily's last actions dominates the tone of the second half of the novel: the reader cannot expect rescue, no matter how easily the word has been bandied about. Lily's death, then, can be greeted with detachment. The reader has not seen any change in circumstances coming; more important, the reader probably would not want any change in Lily's circumstances, because such change would have to come from either Lawrence Selden or Simon Rosedale. At the ending of the book, neither man has been presented as admirable enough to deserve Lily.

Wharton has written a most unusual novel. Instead of becoming devoted to Lily, wanting her to win out over circumstances despite the viciousness of society, readers accept her inevitable denouement. Wharton keeps the reader so distant from Lily—by showing her through the eyes of observers such as Selden who have no insight into her inner workings—that her novel avoids any charge of sentimentality. Wharton escapes being considered a conventional woman writer, and *The House of Mirth* escapes being labeled a "domestic novel"—which it is, through the author's choice of narrative perspective. Because the reader is not asked to rescue Lily through sympathy, the process of reading the novel becomes highly intellectualized; and because Wharton focuses the reader's attention on scenes of word play and language manipulation (such as the "freedom" and "republic of the spirit" interchanges between Lily and Selden), the meaning of the text seems translatable.

Part of the author's irony stems from the fact that there is no simple meaning for the novel, and any reader's attempt to interpret the story's events will be limited to partial summation. *The House of Mirth* is a dark, almost vengeful novel, one of admonition rather than of manners. Its complex message is in some ways so inimical to the reader that one might rather leave it mysterious. *Play by all the rules, regardless of who has made them, or you will end up dead. And, women's lives are meant to be empty and decorative, tapestries of chicanery and adultery and dishonesty; either live them in that mode, or give up any right to be a woman.*

Because *The House of Mirth* was a runaway best-seller, one assumes that Wharton's essentially modernist technique of juxtaposing scenes without heavy explanation enabled readers to find their own meanings.

For every reader who read the novel as one might today, perhaps half a dozen found it a moral warning that the dictates of society must be obeyed—by men as well as women. Lily Bart's story in that reading would be representative of what might happen to anyone outside the pale of convention. Robbed of its gender specificity, Lily's story does fit one of the traditional themes of earlier American literature, that of the outsider, the maverick loner who is doomed to be crushed by the very social forms he or she resists. Perhaps this is the reason so much commentary on the novel seems to omit any mention of gender. Few critics have talked about the double standard, for instance, or about Wharton's greatest irony—that Lily is a virgin when she dies at thirty-one, ill, condemned to penury if not starvation, treated as if she were an immoral and flagrantly sexual fallen woman.

The sometimes harsh criticism of Lily seems to have missed Wharton's greatest irony in a structure of many ironies: if anything, Lily is hardly a character of blame. Though she tries to act on her intentions, though she attempts to be the maverick, she usually succumbs to convention. She might take tea with Selden in his rooms, but she does not sleep with him—or with any other man—anywhere. She might flirtatiously "borrow" money from Gus Trenor, but she keeps the social forms so firmly in place that she does not endanger her reputation at any time (it is Gus's break from convention that endangers her reputation). She might be impatient with the restraints she feels at Mrs. Peniston's, but she is obliging and polite, never troublesome to her icy aunt in any way. She allows Mrs. Peniston to keep her on sporadic allowances, funding which both she and her aunt know is insufficient for her needs, and she accepts criticism with docility and remorse. Lily Bart at twenty-nine, thirty, and thirty-one is hardly treated as if she is the grown niece of a wealthy and presumably loving family.

Such criticism of Lily exists because readers persist in reading *The House of Mirth* as if it were a text "about" things that it is not. It presumes that Lily is a free agent empowered by her family's money to make decisions, but Wharton frequently shows the reader that Lily has no power of any kind, except what her society will lend her because of her immense physical beauty. The reader instead should understand from the start how limited Lily's freedom can be, and read her narrative from the perspective Ellen Moers describes as that of characters of secondary status, characters who have to recognize constraints on travel, education, marriage choices, and adulthood.[24]

Lily, Wharton, and the novel all share in what DuPlessis calls "double consciousness," the state of mind of a marginal or secondary person who yet understands the primary culture's mandates. Straddling two worlds, the marginal but educated character is forced to maintain a delicate balancing act. This is what Lily tries to do when Selden talks about finding a "republic of the spirit." She understands that Selden wants to cross the boundaries of conventional society, and she admires his impulse to do so; but he has ways of making such a move, while she has no money, no power, and no independence. If she is to find her own (or his) republic of the spirit, she will have to have help to make any change. Learning to live with this "double consciousness" is difficult, and many women or minority characters find themselves unable to keep appropriate balance. Their ability to speak in two discourses, to live in two worlds, is often unsettling; and madness or other illness results.[25]

Lily's depression—the slow loss of clear thinking ability, the sleeplessness, the lack of appetite, and the tendency to depressive thoughts—is as much a result of her inability to maintain balance between worlds as it is a physical manifestation. The most debilitating situation in Lily's world as Wharton chooses to present it in the second half of the novel is that no other characters share her insight. Gerty leads an entirely male-identified life, accepting the social script of marriage for beautiful women as given (and discounting her own marriageability because she is not beautiful). Mrs. Peniston sees only the outer social forms and cares for nothing but maintaining those. The only men who might have a glimpse of what Lily is dealing with are those who are themselves marginal—Selden, by reason of his supposed intellectual superiority, and Rosedale, by reason of his definitely marginal ethnic status.

Lily, then, is placed in the same role of isolated and frustrated consciousness that Wharton experienced as a woman attempting to become a writer although her family, friends, husband, and society did not approve that aim—or recognize why that aim was important to Edith Newbold Jones Wharton as person. As Mary Jacobus has described the role of woman writer, "at once within culture and outside it," that writer's role becomes increasingly difficult: to "challenge the terms and work within them."[26] And, if she is skillful enough, she will finally manage to rewrite gender in texts that will become dominant fiction.

DuPlessis points out accurately that "all forms of dominant narrative, but especially romance, are tropes for the sex-gender system as a whole."[27] For Wharton to write an apparent domestic or marriage novel, but so thoroughly subvert the usual plot of such a novel, means that she was clearly participating in the all-important aesthetic activity of critiquing story. It may look as if Lily Bart's story were one of romance, of her being too disdainful of possible mates. The man-woman theme is, however, only a subplot to Lily's real narrative, which is her refusal to lead a life like that of her mother, or Mrs. Peniston, or Bertha Dorset, or Judy Trenor, or Carry Fisher, or Gerty Farish. Wharton's giving Lily this "new" story, one that builds on the reader's expectations and then leads the reader away from those expectations, signals her intention to write the Edna Pontellier story that Kate Chopin created in *The Awakening,* the story of a woman choosing the terms and conditions of her life, not only her suitor.

Just as Edna turns for information about women's choices to her friends, one a mother figure, the other an artist, Lily turns to Selden. Lily's tragedy is to be so thoroughly male-identified at the start of this last phase of her career: by relying on Selden, she "learns" false information, and builds her hopes on mainstream ideology that cannot apply to her as a marginal character. Edna knows better than to turn to any of the men with whom she is involved in the Chopin novel. Lily's seemingly wrong move, turning to Selden, is one of the ways Wharton is able to criticize even the better kinds of that mainstream thinking, but it also signals the reader that Lily has problems besides being so reliant on men's opinions.

The primary reason Lily turns to Selden is that she has no appropriate women to use as counselors. By emphasizing this part of Lily's dilemma as much as she does, Wharton is taking on a very different narrative task than that of merely remodeling the marriage novel: she is writing a type of bildungsroman (appropriate since Lily has remained, through her sexual innocence, a kind of child even at twenty-nine), so the adult models for Lily as character will be of great significance. The adult female models are, obviously, of little use to Lily, because she has already denied the efficacy of their moral systems. Wharton is attempting what DuPlessis calls "a reassessment of the processes of gendering." Instead of fitting Lily's story into a more conventional oedipal narrative—stressing Lily's lack of male aggression, her relationship with her father, her need to be protected and dependent—Wharton shows Lily with a fair amount of that male aggression; with a reasonably good relationship with a father that reads poetry, cares about her, and is modest and self-effacing; and with no need whatsoever to be protected and dependent (except for her financial need, which could have been erased had Mrs. Peniston held true to the bonds of family that her society would have expected). The crux of Lily's instability (in that even when she decides to take action, she wavers and appears unsure) is not so much any failure to be a man as it is a failure of female role models or sources of information. Both Annis Pratt and DuPlessis have noted that many female quest plots (such as those in Virginia Woolf's *To the Lighthouse* and Doris Lessing's *The Four-Gated City*) loop backward to mother-child attachments, or, in the case of stories of artists' development (Kunstlerroman), "may invent an interplay between the mother, the father, and the hero, in a 'relational triangle.'"[28] This description applies well to Wharton's arrangement of narrative elements in *The House of Mirth*.

The risk Wharton runs, by privileging Lily's narrative as the story of a woman who knows what she wants—and, just as important, what she doesn't want—is the loss of both her readership and her critical standing. To make Lily the clear aggressive "hero" and *The House of Mirth* the account of her (failed) efforts to become a woman she admires is to elevate what might be a welcome subplot to the level of the main story. Because readers reflect their culture all too well, in 1905 the story that would have been appropriate for Lily to write and live is the story of finding a "good" husband, a dependable provider who would enable her to find the modicum of social power that was the province of well-placed women characters. Any other narrative becomes implicitly subversive and therefore dangerous—misleading, troublesome, a questioning device rather than a confirming vehicle. Again, DuPlessis notes that fiction during the late nineteenth century repeatedly showed "self-realization and ambition as a female crime."[29] If a woman character was to have a vocation (heaven forbid! as we see in the social reaction to Gerty Farish and her way of living), that vocation would be absolutely separated from heterosexual love. The issue in *The House of Mirth* is not Lily Bart's vocation (although her society takes pleasure in talking about marriage as if it were a woman's vocation; Selden, in fact, uses the word in his initial taunt to Lily). It is the incompatibility of Lily's kind of spirit, of her need to have a quest rather than just a hunt (for a man to marry her), with what her society expects of her as a beautiful woman. Wharton is writing about stereotypes, about the narrowing expectations of social class, about the risks women run whenever they deviate from socially approved norms, and about the responsibilities a culture such as Lily's has toward its powerless members.

Lily's flaw as character is not her indecisiveness, her inability to make up her mind which man she wants to marry and pursue him. It is her being an entirely different kind of woman, an *other* to the social code that governs her life—and that identity demands her death. Wharton chose as her narrative for Lily's highly unconventional life the marriage novel, but in focusing her reader's attention on heterosexual romance she subverted the entire literary structure. *The House of Mirth* as a marriage novel could not contain the spirited Lily Bart because her story was not that of an expectant, waiting young girl. It was the story of a demanding adult woman who, at twenty-nine, thirty, and thirty-one, knows the score full well and wants more from life than diamond bracelets, Coupe Jacques, and even well-furnished houses. As she says with some impatience to Gerty late in the novel:

> You think we live *on* the rich, rather than with them: and so we do, in a sense—but it's a privilege we have to pay for! We eat their dinners, and drink their wine, and smoke their cigarettes, and use their carriages and their opera-boxes and their private cars—yes, but there's a tax to pay

on every one of those luxuries. . . . the girl pays it by tips and cards . . .
and by going to the best dress-makers, and having just the right dress
for every occasion, and always keeping herself fresh and exquisite and
amusing! . . .
> It doesn't sound very amusing, does it? And it isn't—I'm sick to
death of it! And yet the thought of giving it all up nearly kills me—it's
what keeps me awake at night, and makes me so crazy for your strong
tea. (266–67)

There is no question that Lily wants to live well, but she wants to do so
on her own terms. And for a powerless, voiceless woman character at the
turn of the century, there were no such terms in existence. Lily's behavior
was unfeminine, inappropriate, and unseemly. And in society's eyes, her
death was warranted.

nine

The Impossible Suitors

Because Wharton's strategy in *The House of Mirth* is to characterize Lily as marriageable object, to place her at least partly within the plot confines of the novel of marriage, the reader's initial interest in the male characters lies in seeing them as possible suitors for Lily. Caring about Lily means hoping she finds a likely man to marry. Much of the criticism about her as character focuses on her indecisiveness regarding these men, yet Wharton makes very clear that none is a serious candidate for Lily's hand.

Wharton begins with calculated ease. Reserving for Selden the initial role of narrator, Wharton turns her attention to the obvious unsuitability of Percy Gryce. Innocent beyond belief, the sternly moralistic Percy suits his Christian name. Gryce, endowed with his uncle's collection of Americana as well as his family's fortune, is the collector supreme; Lily would be but another acquisition. Wharton concentrates on his shyness, showing it as unbecoming in a man of his financial power, but using his reticence to show Lily's skills at plotting and controlling. Watching Gryce surreptitiously on the train, Lily "organized a method of attack" (17). Their consequent encounter, taking tea and conversing, shows Lily at her most astute ("Some girls would not have known how to manage him. . . . Lily's methods were more delicate" [19]). Although Bertha Dorset takes Gryce on during the Bellomont house party, Lily has no doubt that she can have his proposal before the week is over. Wharton uses Lily's meditation about Gryce, and her situation, to win the reader's sympathy for her protagonist: "She had been bored all the afternoon by Percy Gryce—the mere thought seemed to waken an echo of his droning voice—but she could not ignore him on the morrow, she must follow up her success, must submit to more boredom . . . and all on the bare chance that he might ultimately decide to do her the honour of boring her for life (25)." Remaking herself for the week (Lily must not smoke or play bridge, wear becoming clothes, or understand innuendoes) tires Lily to the point of recalcitrance; she lies to Gryce in order to spend time with Selden, a move that sets Bertha Dorset into action against her. Bertha's anger becomes the cause of Lily's fall from social position. Her first move is to tell Gryce all of Lily's failings, and to misinterpret other of her acts so that they become improprieties: the young collector leaves several days early, in obvious flight from Lily. Judy Trenor warns her friend that Bertha is "dangerous. . . . Bertha's done her work and poisoned him thoroughly" (75). When Lily asks Judy *what* Bertha told Gryce, Judy answers candidly: "Don't ask me—horrors! She seems to have raked up everything. Oh, you know what I mean—of course there isn't anything, *really*. . . . They're all alike, you know: they hold their tongues for years . . . but when their opportunity comes they remember everything" (76). Wharton's pointed insistence on the fabrication of fact, the unscrupulous manipulation of information to serve whatever purposes seem desirable, suggests that the reader must understand that Bertha— like the rest of her society—will stop at nothing to destroy Lily. When Judy shifts from the singular "she," meaning Bertha, to the plural "they," meaning the society in which the three women live, she gives Lily crucial information.

Judy gives her more crucial information in the following scene, when she asks Lily to drive to the station to pick up Gus because she thinks Carry Fisher, the divorcee of the set, has been using these drives to ingratiate herself with him. In Judy's words, Carry had "bled him rather severely," foreshadowing the situation Lily inherits once she has accepted money from Gus's investments. Immediately placed in the same position as Carry, Lily finds herself conscious of Gus's "small dull eyes," features set in unappealing contrast with his "red" and "massive" appearance. She reacts with repugnance (80–81). Wharton's establishing that Lily feels no attraction to Gus, that her business deals with him are only that, makes his insistence that Lily "repay" her debts even more ridiculous. The traumatic overtures Gus makes throughout the first book of the novel, culminating in the late-night scene at his house, serve to increase the reader's sympathy for Lily. Wharton makes clear that Lily does not understand either the social or financial imperatives which motivate Gus. Their crucial dialogue takes place as an interchange of misunderstood language cues, with Gus assuming the role of clear questioner ("I'll tell you what I want: I want to know just where you and I stand. Hang it, the man who pays for the dinner is generally allowed to have a seat at table") and Lily thrown completely off balance by his interrogation ("Pay up? . . . Do you mean that I owe you money?") (145–46).

Just as she has with the dialogue between Selden and Lily, Wharton here uses the characters' language to keep some pretense of neutrality. At first, the reader is almost sympathetic with Gus's demands. He is not a clever man; he understands that money is power, and he wants some return from his investment. When he says to Lily's protest ("If you have brought me here to say insulting things—"), "Don't talk stage-rot. I don't want to insult you. But a man's got his feelings," the reader understands his rudeness. But Wharton extends the scene until it is clear that the naive participant is Lily, and that Gus is using his facade of crudity to frighten and coerce her. He admits as much himself when he says, "Don't stare at me like that—I know I'm not talking the way a man is supposed to talk to a girl—but, hang it, if you don't like it you can stop me quick enough" (146). Even though Gus admits his impropriety (at strange variance with his calling her "Miss Lily" through the scene), he continues his insults. His last speech is unpardonable: "Ah—you'll borrow from Selden or Rosedale—and take your chances of fooling them as you've fooled me! Unless—unless you've settled your other scores already—and I'm the only one left out in the cold!" (146–47).

As Gus's words make clear, in the society Lily holds dear, the unmarried girl is primarily a sexual object. After she is experienced, her value as a marriage partner drops to nothing—although in Lily's case, Gus implies that he wants her even if Selden and Rosedale have already made love to her. One of the frightening aspects of Trenor's assault is his self-righteousness: he has reminded Lily earlier that she is "dodging the rules of the game"; again, that she "ain't playing fair" (145). The social code *he* knows, from his position of wealthy married man, has an established power brokerage that he assumes Lily also knows: she has spent his money, and now she owes him sexual favors. He finds it hard to believe Lily is innocent either of knowledge or of sexual experience, as another of his damning insults implies: "I don't doubt you've accepted as much before—and chucked the other chaps as you'd like to chuck me. I don't care how you settled your score with them—if you fooled 'em I'm that much to the good" (146). Gus will enjoy his sexual rights even more if, by some remote chance, Lily has remained a virgin. Wharton makes her point clearly: the Trenors are among Lily's closest friends.

Lily initially finds Simon Rosedale even more repugnant than she does Trenor, but because he appears throughout the novel first as suitor and then as friend, her response to him changes. Despite Wharton's anti-Semitism, which was regrettably all too common in early modernist fiction, the reader comes to have empathy for Rosedale (and his name becomes more and more appropriate as the narrative moves forward). What is most impressive about Rosedale is that he does have sympathy—and perhaps even love—for Lily, and he is not afraid to show his allegiance to her even after the society he longs to enter has dropped her.

Rosedale speaks a language Lily can understand. When he proposes to her, he phrases his desire as "a plain business statement" (177). He explains that his "character" is such that what he wants he is willing to pay for, and now that he has made his fortune his objective is "the right woman to spend it" (175). There is a touching poignance in Rosedale's plain speaking when he assures Lily that he knows she is "not dead in love" with him, or even "not very fond" of him, but he thinks such a marriage would work.

Rosedale's unconventional proposal is not offensive partly because it is in character, and partly because the reader senses that he does have

Lily Bart's best interests at heart. He says eloquently that he wants her to enjoy her life and be able to avoid the "bothers" her society puts before her. In his terse language, "what I'm offering you is the chance to turn your back on them once for all" (177). By the end of *The House of Mirth*, Lily considers him a friend. Somewhat before, when she does consider marrying him but he refuses her unless she will use Bertha Dorset's letters to gain her place in society back, the reader feels that his response has been, again, in character. In their final scene together, when he is amazed at Lily's working as an apprentice and living in poverty, their friendship finally coalesces. She genuinely appreciates his inarticulate compliment, "Miss Lily, if you want any backing—I like pluck" (293).

George Dorset's "long sallow face and distrustful eyes" are described early in the novel, and Lily is never able to feel anything but a vague pity for Bertha's cuckolded husband. Her unwillingness to allow George to see how unfaithful Bertha has been, and is, is another enigma to her society. In order for George to divorce Bertha, he would need Lily's testimony and support. Once Lily helps Bertha cover up her late-night exploits with Ned Silverton, and allows herself to be used as the focus of the ensuing scandal, she has lost any hope of becoming George's ally. Wharton makes clear that Lily could have played that role: "It was a dreadful hour—an hour from which she emerged shrinking and seared. . . . Her sense of being involved in the crash, instead of merely witnessing it from the road, was intensified by the way in which Dorset, through his furies of denunciation and wild reactions of self-contempt, made her feel the need he had of her, the place she had taken in his life. But for her, what ear would have been open to his cries? And what hand but hers could drag him up again to a footing of sanity and self-respect?" (203).

When Lily agrees that George should see Selden, she puts the quietus on the situation. Selden, both because of his involvement with Bertha and because of his tendency to help keep surface calm, is a safe attorney for George at this unsettled point in his decision-making process. As Wharton points out clearly: "It was in Bertha's interest, certainly, that she had despatched Dorset to consult with Lawrence Selden. . . . It was to Bertha that Lily's sympathies now went out. She was not fond of Bertha

Dorset, but neither was she without a sense of obligation, the heavier for having so little personal liking to sustain it. Bertha had been kind to her" (205). Wharton here involves the reader in classic dramatic irony: the reader knows that Bertha has acted out of no kindness toward Lily, but only to further her own plans. Once Lily forgets Judy Trenor's warning about Bertha, the novel has no course but to destroy Lily.

Wharton gives Lily one last chance to turn the tables on Bertha. After she has become part of the Gormers' crowd, Lily sees George Dorset in passing, and he stops her and pleads with her to help him get a divorce from Bertha: "'you're the only person'—his voice dropped to a whisper—'the only person who knows. . . . I want to be free, and you can free me'" (244). After George's extended plea, Lily again refuses to help him, but the explication of her thoughts that Wharton provides is completely clear. Marrying Dorset is Lily's chance to regain her former position, and more. Lily thinks, "Here was a man who turned to her in the extremity of his loneliness and his humiliation: if she came to him at such a moment he would be hers with all the force of his deluded faith. And the power to make him so lay in her hand—lay there in a completeness he could not even remotely conjecture. Revenge and rehabilitation might be hers at a stroke—there was something dazzling in the completeness of the opportunity" (245).

Wharton's final irony concerning the Dorsets comes immediately after this scene, when the reader finds that Bertha has decided to lower herself and call on Mrs. Gormer. Wharton implies that Lily's days with the Gormers will be numbered because Bertha will wreak her damaging way into their confidences. Even while Lily harbors no anger against Bertha and thinks revenge is beneath her, Wharton shows that Bertha is actively moving toward creating an even more complete downfall for Lily Bart.

Throughout the novel, Wharton provides a number of potential mates for Lily, but she describes them so that the reader takes none of them seriously. Outright physical descriptions mark their inferiority: they are *dull, shy, red, shiny, massive,* or *sallow*. They are also pristine, priggish, already married, or social-climbing. Given Wharton's unappealing gallery, it is no wonder the reader—like Lily—begins to think Lawrence

Selden is her best hope. But under scrutiny, Selden too is objectionable: a reasonably confirmed bachelor, he has little money, a history of affairs with married women, a love of rhetorical games and flirtations, a tendency to make pronouncements and give orders, and a history of running away from confrontation. He likes to be admired, as his relationship with his adoring cousin, Gerty Farish, shows; and many of Wharton's scenes between Lily and Selden reveal his pleasure at being in charge, at having the answers. Wharton makes her intentions about Selden's character clear by never showing him to be sincerely, or seriously, interested in Lily or her welfare. The randomness of their contact—and the explanation for his long absences from the plot—is partly meant to reinforce his lack of consistent interest in her. Selden's concern for Lily, if it exists at all, occurs when she chances to cross his path. He does not arrange his life to make contact with Lily Bart.

Wharton's creation, and manipulation, of Selden may be less than obvious because of the role he plays in parts of the novel as pseudonarrator; but once his place as instrument of narration is understood, his role of suitor becomes less believable. Another of Wharton's intentions becomes obvious as the reader meets, evaluates, and dismisses each of the other male characters. If Lily's role is to marry, surely there should be suitors more acceptable than these. The very lack of suitable candidates is one clue to the fact that *The House of Mirth,* finally, is not meant to be a novel of marriage. It is instead a novel about women's choices; and when Lily comes to Selden on the last night of her life, moved by some inscrutable purpose that involves Bertha's letters to him, her central speech is not about whether she is going to be married. (His question to her, however, does fix on that issue.) It is rather a speech about Lily Bart as person, Lily Bart as woman without space or purpose, Lily Bart as failure in social—and, more seriously, human—terms.

> I have tried hard—but life is difficult, and I am a very useless person. I can hardly be said to have an independent existence. I was just a screw or a cog in the great machine I called life, and when I dropped out of it I found I was of no use anywhere else. What can one do when one finds that one only fits into one hole? One must get back to it or be

thrown out into the rubbish heap—and you don't know what it's like
in the rubbish heap! (308)

Seeing this speech as the core of Lily's personal search makes
Wharton's structure of *The House of Mirth* less surprising, because most
of the novel is not about Lily's search for a husband. Except for the early
scenes with Percy Gryce, Lily is seldom working toward achieving a marriage. She is more often helping her friends, deflecting courtship language
and acts, or bargaining with her own troublesome economic fate. In
short, Lily Bart is trying to lead an all-too-human life, finding some purpose in her existence, keeping her life in order, and feeling increasingly
burdened with the machinations of deceit she sees around her. Although
many of her problems are gender-specific, a good part of Lily's life is
shared by all people, women and men, who must consider issues of fi-
nances, family, friendship, and self-worth throughout their daily lives.
Lily Bart gains memorable distinction in that, in Wharton's fictional
world, she becomes a thoroughly human character.

ten
_____

Daisy Miller and
The House of Mirth

One of the literary models Wharton was working from, and against, as she refigured the innocent American ingenue in Lily Bart was the enigmatic—and perhaps unsatisfactorily drawn—Daisy Miller, from Henry James's novella of that name. An important American fiction since its publication in 1878, *Daisy Miller* gave to literature the prototype of the innocent American girl. James frequently worked with the theme of innocence (identified with the American nationality) usurped by the sophisticated corruption of the Old World. Sometimes the American innocent was female; occasionally, male. The stable part of the paradigm was that American innocence was set against the deceiving malevolence of European characters and culture, as in his *The American*, *The Portrait of a Lady*, *Roderick Hudson*, *The Wings of the Dove*, *The Ambassadors*, *The Golden Bowl*, and other fictions. Of all James's gallery of American naïfs, Daisy Miller became the most memorable. As the icon of bluff, outspoken (and thereby rash) self-confidence, going her own impetuous and imperious way, Daisy combined the freshness and coarseness of the wildflower for which she was named in her conquest of European society.

Sandra M. Gilbert and Susan Gubar see Wharton's Lily Bart and the social context that comprises *The House of Mirth* as drawn from a number of late nineteenth-century novels—Kate Chopin's 1899 *The Awakening*, Rider Haggard's 1887 *She*, and Olive Schreiner's 1883 *The Story of an African Farm*.

Rather than conveying the notion of sexual naiveté, these novels put forth women characters who have to make mature decisions, sometimes at the sacrifice of their "good" name or position in society. According to Gilbert and Gubar, the dominant literary tradition for these works is the depiction of the femme fatale, the woman as sexual risk, set against the image of the woman as heartless; they see that Wharton's choices of both the character of Lily Bart and her situations throughout the novel are in ironic counterpoint to these more visible literary patterns of the time. They speak to the fact that *The House of Mirth* is perhaps as much a comment on Thorstein Veblen's *The Theory of the Leisure Class*—as well as Charlotte Perkins Gilman's *Women and Economics: A Study of the Economic Relation between Men and Women as a Factor in Social Evolution*, published in 1898, a year earlier than the Veblen book—as it is a depiction of the beautiful husband-hunting siren. Lily Bart is, in fact, the reverse of that stereotyped woman: she sabotages herself as she holds out for a husband she can love, rather than marry someone to be her household provider. (As Gilbert and Gubar accurately point out, the character of Bertha Dorset, Lily's antagonist, bears some similarity to the Bertha Mason Rochester of *Jane Eyre*, a combination of the femme fatale and the woman of destruction: "sexually voracious, dissipated, profligate, and duplicitous".)[30]

The character of Lily Bart, however, while she may be some ironic statement about the supposed power of late nineteenth-century women, stands in clear outline as the least powerful of Wharton's women characters. Everything about Lily at the time the novel opens is ineffectual—if not simply wrong. She is twenty-nine years old, eleven years past her debut: her society is watching, counting, wondering. Lily has made the supreme mistake of allowing all that time to pass without snaring a husband. Her society understands time as a linear progression; it has no sympathy for her more cyclic sense of events and human understanding. In contrast to James's Daisy Miller, who is simply young and marriageable,

Lily Bart exists in a precarious position: defined as young and virginal, qualities necessary for her worth on the marriage market, she is nearly thirty. Once her age passes the reasonable demarcations of definition, can her society believe that her virginity has not also been transformed with the passing of time?

Both *Daisy Miller* and *The House of Mirth* open with the scene of the male observer character—Winterbourne and Selden—scrutinizing the protagonist and admiring her fresh beauty. Both fictions use the strategy of making the reader understand that women are marketable products, and that the male figures in any fiction are the purchasers. Although the reader understands this convention of the romance (marriage) novel, James presents Daisy Miller as somehow immune from Winterbourne's scrutiny. Her young brother Randolph introduces her as "an American girl," and Winterbourne's observation echoes that impersonality, the girl as a generic type. For all the detail James provides, Winterbourne's summation is in the plural: "The young lady meanwhile had drawn near. She was dressed in white muslin, with a hundred frills and flounces, and knots of pale-coloured ribbon. She was bare-headed; but she balanced in her hand a large parasol, with a deep border of embroidery; and she was strikingly, admirably pretty. 'How pretty they are!' thought Winterbourne."[31] Nearly three pages of conversation elapse before Winterbourne learns the American girl's name ("Annie P. Miller"), so that much of this initial description repeats the locution "American girl" unremittingly. Woven throughout the detail of James's description is Winterbourne's indecision about what role the girl is playing: "Never, indeed, since he had grown old enough to appreciate things, had he encountered a young American girl of so pronounced a type as this. Certainly she was very charming; but how ducedly sociable! Was she simply a pretty girl from New York State—were they all like that, the pretty girls who had a good deal of gentlemen's society? Or was she also a designing, an audacious, an unscrupulous young person?" (143–44).

In Winterbourne's confusion, James expresses the dilemma that Wharton's male characters face—but do not express—in their decisions about Lily Bart in *The House of Mirth*. James has more fun with the dilemma: he describes Winterbourne's state of mind with heavy irony, giving him platitudes as conventional and unhelpful as those that come from Daisy Miller's own lips. This is the continuation of the monologue above:

> Miss Daisy Miller looked extremely innocent. Some people had told him that, after all, American girls were exceedingly innocent; and others had told him that, after all, they were not. He was inclined to think Miss Daisy Miller was a flirt—a pretty American flirt. He had never, as yet, had any relations with young ladies of this category. He had known, here in Europe, two or three women—persons older than Miss Daisy Miller, and provided, for respectability's sake, with husbands—who were great coquettes—dangerous, terrible women, with whom one's relations were liable to take a serious turn. But this young girl was not a coquette in that sense; she was very unsophisticated; she was only a pretty American flirt. Winterbourne was almost grateful for having found the formula that applied to Miss Daisy Miller. (144)

Winterbourne's seeming propriety is a sham. James has made clear that the cautious Winterbourne is having an affair with an older woman, and that his affair is the reason he stays in Europe. Far from the innocent American, Winterbourne has become the European sophisticate he alludes to here. But he is honest in admitting that he cannot decipher the intention behind Daisy Miller's conversation; and in his playing language games (What is the difference, for example, between a "flirt" and a "coquette," and why should Winterbourne feel reassured that Daisy is "only" a flirt?), he lulls himself into thinking he is in control of their relationship. Winterbourne's facade of control is exactly what Wharton borrows for the character of Selden in *The House of Mirth*. Another veteran of affairs with married women, another jaded observer who fails to believe in a young lady's innocence, Selden, like Winterbourne, participates in life linguistically rather than emotionally.

James's narrative plot line is a traditional romance, as Daisy Miller uses her Roman suitor to make Winterbourne jealous. The novella suggests that her acts are intentional, always under the pretense that she does not understand the European cultural conventions. The remarkable scene of Mrs. Walker's carriage, and the controversy about whether or not Daisy should be walking with men on the Pincio, parallel Wharton's giving Lily Bart the dubious distinction of being the center of attention at the Brys' tableaux: under the gaze of hostile and predatory social observers, each woman becomes a mirage, an icon for whatever meaning society wants to draw from her self. James's final irony is having Daisy Miller and her suitor Giovanelli hide behind Daisy's parasol so that Winterbourne believes they are kissing in public. Wharton's similar scene in *The House of Mirth* occurs as Selden sees Lily Bart leaving the Trenor house late at night, and suspects that she has been making love with her friend's husband. In each case, the male observer (who is also, of course, a possible suitor) jumps to erroneous conclusions and leaves the scene and the woman character who is in need of support—with nothing but circumstantial evidence.

As a result of each precipitous action, Daisy Miller and Lily Bart are confirmed in a downward spiral that leads eventually to death. Daisy Miller continues her flagrant public courtship with Giovanelli, still hoping Winterbourne will understand that she is trying to make him jealous. Lily Bart continues trying to save herself, taking on whatever projects are offered in the hope of keeping the financial disaster that looms in bounds. Yet each narrative continues the facade of defining both Winterbourne and Selden as observers, and what action the reader does see of them is their wrangling mentally with the question of what each woman means. Meanwhile, both Daisy and Lily endure the insults and ravages of the polite societies to which they belong, pretending to enjoy their outsider roles as they continue to play out their somewhat defiant characterizations.

James shows the reader Daisy's face when Mrs. Walker turns her back to her, refusing to say good-bye; and when she taunts Winterbourne with the notion that she is engaged to Giovanelli. But the climax of their language duel comes at night, when Winterbourne finds Daisy at the Coliseum and tells her in effect that he doesn't care what kind of girl she is, whether or not she is engaged. In return, "'I don't care,' said Daisy, in a little strange tone, 'whether I have Roman fever or not!'" (190). Daisy's death wish is an index of her deep feeling for the unknowing

Winterbourne, whose name has indicated throughout that he will never respond in any positive way. His icy ("stiff") attention to proprieties has alienated the reader, and his bemused attention to Daisy on her death bed, as she dies from the dreaded Roman fever, seems characteristic of his failure to become involved in any meaningful way with the American girl, the naïf who is so trapped in her predictable identity.

Daisy, like Lily Bart, shares those reprehensible traits of candor, outspokenness, and honesty. These personality traits are among those that make Lily an ineffectual "girl"—she speaks too directly, she cuts Sim Rosedale instead of being nice to him, she loses Percy Gryce when she spends time with Selden rather than the younger suitor. Wharton uses Lily's female friends to point out the inappropriateness of Lily's honesty, and reinforces their pattern of emphasis through Lily's own acts. As Judy Trenor laments, "Lily, I can't make you out. . . . you'll never do anything if you're not serious!" (75). The sympathy readers have for Lily Bart differs from that they may feel for Daisy because Wharton's narration makes plain how willful Lily's behavior is. Her losses are the result of clear decision. James's method of narration for his story of Daisy Miller leaves more to the imagination of the reader and gives Winterbourne as narrator more control over what the reader thinks about Daisy herself. As Winterbourne is confused, so too is the reader.

Daisy and Lily share more than their flowerlike names as they move toward the denouement of each story. Willful speech becomes willful act, at least in the case of Daisy's behavior. Disregarding the threat of Roman fever, Daisy flaunts her Roman suitor's attention in the most conspicuous of places—and as a result of her spending time in the moonlit Coliseum, she does catch the dreaded fever. Just as willful in some respects is Lily's decision to go it alone, to do what she must do to live independently, cut off from the people who might have been able to help her. Her failure to make use of Bertha Dorset's letters—even after Rosedale has suggested that using them is the only way to match Bertha's accumulated power and vengeance—means that she is speechless, in effect, when she goes to see Selden for the last time. When she throws the letters into his fire, she becomes voiceless as well as powerless. Her disdain to play the same game others play marks the culmination of her ineffectual behavior.

Lily goes voiceless to her death. From Daisy's death bed, however, comes her message to Winterbourne that she had not been engaged, her explanation that she was not what he had come to think, but rather what she had been at the time of their first meeting. James expands the structure of the novella to add the scene in which Giovanelli confirms Daisy's message, that she had been innocent to the end. What remains with Winterbourne, however, despite Daisy's attempt to reach him, is his memory of "Daisy Miller and her mystifying manners" (192). And he seems content to live with that unresolved mystery as he returns to Geneva, once more dividing his time between his studies and his "very clever foreign lady."

The impression Daisy Miller and her life have made on Winterbourne has been negligible—even though the innocent girl has died as a result of the games necessary in international courtship rituals. Wharton's concluding her novel with Lily's death shows both her appropriation of James's narrative pattern, and her deviation from it. Even though Selden has decided that he does love Lily and is rushing to tell her so (an ending that might have occurred as well in *Daisy Miller*), the reader does not believe that Selden has changed, that he really understands what has been happening in Lily's life.

In fact, much of the rationale for the last chapter of *The House of Mirth* is that Selden is trying to "prove" Lily's innocence, defined at this point in the novel as financial integrity rather than sexual. By deciphering what Lily has done with her inheritance, Selden can decide what kind of person Lily has become. How she has spent her money determines Lily's morality, or lack of moral stance. Wharton's devastating narrative control here is at odds with James's more predictable conclusion of *Daisy Miller*. Winterbourne simply runs down, turns back to old behaviors, and continues his eventless life as it was before his encounter with Daisy Miller. James does not pretend that Daisy Miller's death makes any important impression on Winterbourne—again, beyond some interest in her language, as he explains to his aunt. Wharton, however, is shaping Selden into a different kind of person during the last chapter of *The*

House of Mirth. Selden moves from his passive cynicism to direct invasion. There, in the room in which the dead woman's body lies, only minutes after Selden thought he was coming to claim that woman as his bride, he invades every detail of her life, taking this intimate knowledge as his right. What excuse for his scrutiny Gerty provides is flimsy: what could exist in Lily's room that would dismay the doctor or the police? Under the guise of setting Lily's life in order, then, Selden opens correspondence, drawers, and checkbooks with an equanimity that sends chills through the reader. Wharton deftly contrasts Lily's purchasing Bertha's correspondence to Selden, but not reading it, and finally sacrificing the power it could have given her against Bertha; with Selden's absorption of Lily's correspondence, his needing to justify her life on its terms. Lily is above wanting to know details of Selden's past life. Selden cannot make any commitment to Lily—even in her death—without checking through everything he can lay his hands on.

Wharton spends several paragraphs showing the conflict within Selden as he sees that Lily has written to Trenor. He acknowledges that he is the person with her in death only by chance ("After all, what did he know of her life?"), but rather than respecting that obvious impasse, he rushes in to proclaim that the place of caretaker is his by virtue of "their last hour together, the hour when she herself had placed the key in his hand." But immediately the jealous Selden thinks, "Yes, but what if the letter to Trenor had been written afterward?" (340). Less than a page later, Selden is indulging in the self-congratulatory reverie that makes any mourning for Lily Bart a mockery. What Selden is remembering as he literally stands beside the recently alive body is how well he behaved as lover, how much he and Lily Bart had shared. Wharton's long novel makes all too clear that whatever has been between Lawrence Selden and Lily Bart the reader has seen: that there has been very little, except wordplay, sophistry, and absence. The self-congratulation of Selden's last thoughts is a bitter counterpoint to the nearly emotionless state of James's Winterbourne, and readers who know both characters must prefer the latter.

Winterbourne accepts Daisy's death as a sad loss. He wonders whether she did care for him, but he does not pretend that his life has changed as a result of his knowing her. Selden, on the other hand, for all his distance and lack of involvement when Lily obviously has needed him—or if not him, someone well placed in their society—sees much of his past as colored with his passion for the now-dead woman. He can play the role of the sorrowing lover for a long time, and that mourning will help insulate him from other prospective involvements. Although Selden wants to play the role of the bereft lover, Wharton will not allow him to do so without losing whatever credibility he had as the narrative observer figure. Her indictment is severe, particularly when the reader notices how closely modeled on *Daisy Miller* is the Wharton novel—until its ending.

Perhaps another James's novel also contributed to Wharton's 1905 rebuttal of the conventions of romance. In 1903 James had published *The Ambassadors*, a novel which sold very poorly but received wide critical acclaim. In the character of Lambert Strether, James moved beyond any hint of conventional romance in creating the observer content to stay observer. When Strether renounces Europe and Maria Gostrey, James reifies the renunciation with Strether's simple, and unequivocal, explanation: "all the same I must go. . . . To be right."[32] When Maria tries to make him talk further, this dialogue occurs:

> "That, you see, is my only logic. Not, out of the whole affair, to have got anything for myself."
> She thought. "But, with your wonderful impressions, you'll have got a great deal."
> "A great deal"—he agreed. "But nothing like *you*. It's you who would make me wrong!" (375)

James's creation of the self-sufficient man, the man immune to the lures of conventional romance even with the most wonderful of women partners, did much to change the fabric of the romance novel. Imputing the bravest self understanding to Strether, James defined the novel as the narrative of a dominant consciousness—usually male. Wharton might have come to this pattern eventually, particularly when she undertook to describe the consciousness of women characters, but at this early point in her writing career, she had little choice but to write fiction that was recognizable in form. James's *The Ambassadors* gave Wharton further characterization of the distant yet not unloving male, a superior man, to whom women were drawn—ineffectually. Strether as nay-sayer was a kind of character Wharton did not want to include in her fiction, but his presence reinforced what she was daily observing in her own life and society. Men could exist—economically, professionally, emotionally—on their own, whereas women were dependent on males (as husbands, lovers, business advisers, creators of the social code). Lily Bart was a sorry sacrifice to a system which Wharton could understand all too well but was powerless to change. As a woman herself, she had no recourse but to live within its patterns, and to pretend women's roles were equal to those of men. That they were not, and would never be, was one reason she grew angry reading James's important—and all too realistic—fictions. It was logical that she would in some ways "answer" the patterns he created in his narrative re-creation of his world.

Twenty-five years after publishing *The House of Mirth*, Wharton wrote in a letter to William Gerhardi, a young novelist, about the entire social form of courtship and marriage, a form that remained much more life-directing for women than it was for men. "*Why* do the young still marry? . . . I suppose it's a case of a purely obsolete and fetishistic act being performed automatically by a generation which has completely forgotten what it meant."[33] Wharton's skepticism about the social form of marriage fits into the anger she conveys throughout *The House of Mirth*. Had Lily Bart not been expected to marry, had she not been subject to the whim of every marriageable man in her society, she might have come to find her own self, her own promise, her own sense of being separate from those empty social forms that ruled her very existence. Once freed from the tyranny of marriage, Wharton herself could become the person she needed to learn to be. If there was any mourning to be done for the character of Lily Bart, it was never the role of Selden to undertake it; it was eventually the role of Edith Wharton, novelist and professional woman, who by the time of the publication of *The House of Mirth* had realized who she was, and in what directions her talent could take her—and was happy, secretly, to give to Scribner's, for the use of her friend Henry James, the sum of eight thousand dollars from the royalties of the novel that owed so much—directly or indirectly—to his fiction.[34] Acting as an irritant to Wharton's creative process, James's *Daisy Miller* may have helped to form Wharton's first distinctive, and unexpectedly political, novel, *The House of Mirth*.

eleven

Edith Wharton and
The House of Mirth

T*he House of Mirth* is often considered a criticism of the inhumanity of acquisitive Victorian society. Because Wharton was thought to be a novelist of manners whose main interest was in describing cultural milieu and the effect of society on characters, some readers tended to read her work with an almost historical interest. The life and times of remote, wealthy New Yorkers hardly warrants the level of interest this novel has captured for eighty-five years, however: that interest stems from readers' responses to the character, and plight, of Lily Bart. As Wharton explained in *A Backward Glance*, her 1934 autobiography: "In what aspect could a society of irresponsible pleasure-seekers be said to have, on the "old woe of the world," any deeper bearing than the people composing such a society could guess? The answer was that a frivolous society can acquire dramatic significance only through what its frivolity destroys. Its tragic implication lies in its power of debasing people and ideals. The answer, in short, was my heroine Lily Bart."[35] As Wharton knew even in 1905, it is the well-drawn, believable character that makes literature have any import for readers.

Although *The House of Mirth* becomes the novel of Lily Bart, it is also the novel of her society, because without the confinement of those prevalent social codes, Lily's psychological and material life would be very different. Lily has accepted the ideology of her wealthy society; she too believes that her role in life is to be the beautiful ornament who spends her husband's fortune on superior things. Good taste is one of her talents, and proving that she has an exquisite sensibility, one of her chief occupations. Wharton clearly establishes how integral a part of her wealthy society Lily is in her early dialogue with Selden. When, in answer to her lament that she envies him his flat, he points out that Gerty Farish, his cousin, lives alone and is self-sufficient, Lily replies automatically and impolitely, "she has a horrid little place, and no maid, and such queer things to eat. Her cook does the washing and the food tastes of soap." (7).

Not exactly apropos the subject at hand, Lily continues, "we're so different, you know: she likes being good, and I like being happy." In the scenes at Bellomont that follow directly, Wharton defines Lily's "happy" in terms of physical beauty and comfort. Going upstairs to bed, she looks back down into the shadowed hall where "tall clumps of flowering plants were grouped against a background of dark foliage in the angles of the walls . . . and the light from the great central lantern overhead shed a brightness on the women's hair and struck sparks from their jewels as they moved" (25). Wharton tells the reader that "such scenes delighted Lily . . . they gratified her sense of beauty and her craving for the external finish of life."

Lily's anguish that follows, when she realizes that she has lost three hundred dollars playing bridge, is voiced in this same language of comparative ways of life. "To be herself, or a Gerty Farish. As she entered her bedroom, with its softly-shaded lights, her lace dressing-gown lying across the silken bedspread, her little embroidered slippers before the fire, a vase of carnations filling the air with perfume, and the last novels and magazines lying uncut on a table beside the reading-lamp, she had a vision of Miss Farish's cramped flat, with its cheap conveniences and hideous wall-papers" (25). Throughout the novel, Wharton reinforces this aspect of Lily's belief system. Learning to live apart from the beauty and elegance of the wealthy and tasteful is to be a major readjustment for Lily Bart.

So far as the outcome of the novel is concerned, Wharton's emphasis on Lily as intrinsic part of her society makes her disinheritance by Mrs. Peniston a more important plot element than all of Bertha Dorset's duplicity. Wharton links those happenings together, in some sense, but it is after the reading of Mrs. Peniston's will that Lily seems most affected by the specter of change in her life. In a quietly dramatic scene, the audience of relatives clusters about the heiress, Grace Julia Stepney (Mrs. Peniston's namesake), while leaving Lily Bart completely alone, a situation Wharton emphasizes. "Lily stood apart from the general movement, feeling herself for the first time utterly alone. No one looked at her, no one seemed aware of her presence; she was probing the very depths of insignificance" (223). As Lily recovers her self-possession and crosses the room to congratulate Grace, Wharton again stresses Lily's isolation: "The other ladies had fallen back at her approach, and a space created itself about her. It widened as she turned to go, and no one advanced to fill it up. She paused a moment, glancing about her, calmly taking the measure of her situation." Though Lily appears to be in control, Wharton signals that her protagonist has no way of knowing what this change in her social status entails. All her complaints about Mrs. Peniston's dour house, her disgust at the processes of cleaning, her impatience with the quality of the meals, are no longer relevant: Lily will be living elsewhere, in lodgings much less tasteful, and in circumstances far beneath any she has known in her lifetime.

Like Lily, the reader of *The House of Mirth* has become so accustomed to evidences of wealth and elegance that reading the novel is almost impossible without acknowledging the importance of this expensive way of life. The shades of Wharton's characters' appreciations are subtle, often determined by hierarchies of suitability. At the wedding celebration, Lily and Gerty respond much more positively, for instance, to the "exquisite white sapphire" from Percy Gryce than to the "diamond pendant—it's as big as a dinner-plate!" from Simon Rosedale (90). And as this scene shows, the setting for a jewel is often as important as the stone itself. Lily is entranced by the whole display, as Wharton points out: "Lily's heart gave an envious throb as she caught the refraction of light from their surfaces—the milky gleam of perfectly matched pearls, the flash of rubies relieved against contrasting velvet, the intense blue rays of sapphires kindled into light by surrounding diamonds. . . . The glow of the stones warmed Lily's veins like wine. More completely than any other expression of wealth they symbolized the life she longed to lead, the life of fastidious aloofness and refinement in which every detail should have the finish of a jewel, and the whole form a harmonious setting to her own jewellike rareness" (90).

The distinctions between artists, evident in the Brys' tableaux, complement the reader's direction: only the initiated, only the tasteful, understand such nuances. And after establishing these premises throughout most of the novel, Wharton's sudden harsh description of Lily's boarding house parlour, which is "peacock blue," with "bunches of dried pampas grass, and discoloured steel engravings of sentimental episodes" has terrific impact. It is one thing for Lily to complain that her room in Mrs. Peniston's house is dour and shadowy. The point was that she lived in the whole house, and ate dignified and nourishing meals in the candle-lit dining room, served by deferential, obliging servants. Now that she has no choice of residence, and lives in a hall bedroom (a "narrow room, with blotched wall-paper and shabby paint") in a boarding house with a "blistered brown stone front, the windows draped with discoloured lace" in a marginal part of town, her former accommodations seem palatial. She abhors the Rogers' statuette on the console, the Pompeian decoration of the muddy vestibule, and the heavy fumes of the basement dinner table (293). She can hardly down the fried eggs and coffee brought to her room in the morning, or the meals taken in the dimly lit basement, surrounded by strangers all too accustomed to such dining. Wharton's details make clear Lily's pain. So entrenched has she been in the world of wealth, so conditioned to think in its patterns and to accept its values as hers, that being forced to leave that world—and its comfortable environs—is the blow that leads to her precipitous decline.

Wharton makes the reader understand the effect of these changes on Lily by having the usually brusque Rosedale voice his objections. This boarding house parlour is the scene of his last visit to Lily, which he makes before going abroad for several months. It is doubly ironic that Rosedale, whose own taste and discrimination have often been questioned during the course of the novel, speaks the emphatic line, "My goodness—you can't go on living here!" Wharton turns his outcry to double advantage by having Lily misunderstand him and reply that she may be able to afford this house if she can find more work. Rosedale continues, "your being in a place like this is a damnable outrage. I can't talk of it calmly" (298).

Perhaps more debilitating than her living circumstances are Lily's experiences at working. (Wharton uses Rosedale's opinions in the same scene to underscore resentment in that area as well, when Rosedale says, "Out of work—out of work! What a way for you to talk! The idea of your having to work—it's preposterous. . . . It's a farce—a crazy farce.") By using Rosedale as her spokesman, Wharton conveys some sense of real injustice at Lily's position. Reared as she has been, all her efforts to exist without the help of her rich family and friends are not only degrading; they are futile. Lily cannot make it on her own: she is untrained, unaware, unprepared—both intellectually and emotionally. She has neither the skills nor the hardihood to make her own living in the marginal economic world.

The scenes in Regina's hat shop show the distraught Lily, ashamed of her ineptitude, worried by her failures. Her work experiences are catastrophic emotionally. Rather than being the flattered beauty of her set, sought after, praised, admired for her tact and taste, now Lily is just another female in the labor force. In these new social circumstances, her only identity is what she produces. What she can *do* is the world's means of judging her worth, not how she looks or what she knows. When her forewoman says with asperity that all the spangles have been sewn on crookedly, Lily responds as if she had been lashed. Her face burns with vexation not only because of her lack of skill, but because of the "titter" that passes among the other twenty women in the workroom. Lily's pride is deeply hurt: "She knew she was an object of criticism and amusement to the other work-women." She had hoped to find friends here; and one of her early dreams had been "to be received as their equal, and perhaps before long to show herself their superior by a special deftness of touch, and it was humiliating to find that, after two months of drudgery, she still betrayed her lack of early training" (284–85). When Lily loses her job in

April, she has no place to turn—and the failure she has been at trimming hats is her pervasive self-image. It is this characterization of Lily as failure that gives *The House of Mirth* such impact. Lily has fallen from the highest confidence—when, at the Van Osburgh's wedding, she planned her own marriage "within the year"—to her humbling realization that she cannot earn even a meager living for herself. Lily's depression under these traumatic circumstances becomes plausible.

Although Wharton gives the reader much information during the first book of the novel, the heart of the story may lie in the second. One of Wharton's early titles was "The Year of the Rose," a phrase that suggests the brevity of the life of a flower, and that a year may be a significant demarcation. From the September of the novel's opening scene, with Lily taking tea in Selden's flat, to the following autumn, when Rosedale turns back Lily's acceptance of his earlier proposal, one year elapses—and in that amount of time Lily has made the full turn. She has changed from the much-courted member of the right set to the disinherited, lonely woman who has no home, no suitors, and no place in society. With Lily's travels in Europe during the winter comes the most obvious of Bertha Dorset's attacks, turning Lily off the yacht as if she were somehow shamed rather than wronged. With the news of that scandal, Mrs. Peniston changes her will, and Lily begins living the downward spiral that found her so bereft of help of any kind.

The second partial year of Lily's story includes her attempt to find work, with her death occurring at the close of that experience. This part of the narrative seems necessary to allow Wharton to pose the question of "success" or "failure," a recurring theme in much of her early fiction. Lily had always thought of herself as an immense success. She finds it incredible that she is reduced to such poverty, such friendlessness, such lack of options. Wharton had surveyed that evanescent line marking what society meant by success and failure in both her 1899 story, "A Cup of Cold Water," and her 1903 novel, *Sanctuary*. Her working with the terms suggests that she was curious about society's investment of meaning, society's power to judge, when the person to whom the terms were applied might define them differently.

In "A Cup of Cold Water," a narrative of a socially ambitious but

poor young banker in love with elegant Fifth Avenue life, Wharton describes a society much like that which surrounds Lily Bart. Woburn is a
realist. He views the beautiful women (the products of "participating in
the most expensive sports, eating the most expensive food and breathing
the most expensive air") as "costly." Caught in embezzlement, he hides
out in a small hotel and witnesses a young woman's suicide attempt. Saving her life, he convinces her that her life is not a failure, that she has not
failed so long as she has "breath to try again."[36]

A more complex use of the word "success" occurs in *Sanctuary*,
when the interrogation—"What do you call success? It means so many
different things"[37]—comes from Kate Ormsby Peyton, the self-
sacrificing mother whose aim is to break her son's engagement to
Clemence Verney. Verney answers the question bluntly, and wrongly,
but she does so to show Mrs. Peyton that she understands her opposi-
tion. At the end of *Sanctuary*, Verney is alive—though no longer engaged. By the time Selden assumes his position of worldly-wise, morally
superior man in *The House of Mirth*, asking the same question,
Wharton has realized all the deft possibilities inherent in language play.
Selden thinks he is giving Lily sophisticated wisdom when he says that
success is freedom, freedom from "everything—from money, from poverty, from ease and anxiety, from all the material accidents" (72–73). If
ever a protagonist was buried under unexpected "material accidents," it
is Lily Bart; saying one should be free from their existence does not act
as a preventative. And Selden's glib but contradictory pairing of nouns
(*money* and *poverty, ease* and *anxiety*) fails to communicate any serious
intentionality to Lily. What, in fact, does Selden "mean"? Lily longed to
know freedom from poverty, as her last haunted thoughts during those
sleepless nights prove. In the context of Lily's long hegira to disillusion-
ment, Selden's language quips are sillier than they appear on the surface.

The irony, then, of Wharton's having Selden tell the final chapter
in Lily's narrative becomes almost unbearable when the reader remembers his earlier vapidity. Rosedale's exclamation at the circumstances of
Lily's depressed life, his dismay at her living conditions, are genuine.
Contrasting *his* speech with that of Selden reduces the latter's effective-
ness even further; and Wharton sustains that contrast by opening the

last chapter with Selden viewing that same unsuitable boarding house through the rosy glow of his early-morning infatuation. "The sunlight slanted joyously down Lily's street, mellowed the blistered house-front, gilded the paintless railings of the door-step, and struck prismatic glories from the panes of her darkened window" (324). Wharton's irony is relentless. Climbing the three flights of steps, Selden sees the sunlight pouring into her "small bare room," a room that holds only a few traces of luxury—and little else that was Lily's. In Selden's eyes, however, the stark poverty of the room is idealized instead of seen as the obstacle it was to her maintaining her beauty and her health. Wharton has lavished earlier descriptions on Lily's well-appointed bedrooms; the reader knows how important beautiful surroundings were to her. By allowing the reader to forget the aesthetic side of Lily, Wharton emphasizes how false a story Selden is creating during this last retrospective view. Selden, in effect, "translates" the facts of Lily's existence into a narrative which *he* finds palatable.

The reader returns to the question of the final chapter no matter what critical approach motivates the reading. By allowing Selden to finish the tale, as he had begun it; by allowing his language to shape and even create the last scene, which includes the reader's last glimpse of Lily; what has Wharton gained? She has, perhaps, gained a seemingly objective telling of what might have been a sentimental story, a beautiful woman dead because of poverty, depression, and general loss of identity and purpose. But the "objectivity" of Selden's telling is not really that; it rather is an elevation of the character of Selden to protagonist. The power of "telling story" lies both in the control of narrative and in the visible, and oral, foregrounding of the narrator. Wharton has given Selden all this power—but she has also undermined the authority of his position because she has made him a player in the narrative. His integral role in the story necessarily colors his view of it. If Selden maintains objectivity, readers will mistrust him. If he exonerates himself (as he does), readers will dislike him. If he admits to complicity and failed purpose, readers will only agree with his self-disgust.

If Wharton's gains are minimal, she must have had other reasons for ending the novel as she did. Perhaps she has hidden behind the tour de force of this strangely obtuse male narrator, and convinced herself as well as her readers that *The House of Mirth* is some remote fantasy, certainly not a narrative connected with her own experience. Yet many of the central issues of Lily's narrative are also issues that threatened to destroy Wharton's own life—at least her life as writer. As Cynthia Wolff says, "Lily's tale was not unrelated to many of the problems Edith Wharton had experienced in her own life."[38] She recounts Edith Jones's unusually cold and formal relationship with her mother, Lucretia, who was thirty-eight when Edith was born, many years after the two boys who constituted the "planned" family, and Edith's personal insecurity as a result of what she felt as rejection. Her wanting to be a writer met with family disapproval. Her failing to marry Harry Stevens, to whom she was engaged in 1883, because of his mother's disapproval of her, and her general *difference* from the wealthy society into which she had been born, caused even further rejection by her mother. R. W. B. Lewis describes some of Lucretia Jones's efforts to interest Teddy Wharton, the eligible Boston bachelor, in Edith, and their engagement was announced in March of 1885, with a wedding quickly following in April. As Lewis notes, some sense of Lucretia's attitude toward Edith might be drawn from the fact that the engraved wedding invitations "failed to mention Edith's name."[39]

The long history of sexual maladjustment, and the eventual illnesses and breakdowns of both Teddy and Edith Wharton are often recounted, but such history goes beyond the narrative of Lily Bart in *The House of Mirth*. Never "successful" in her quest for marriage, Lily instead faces her death. It may be too much of a literary convention to describe that death, as Wolff does, as "a kind of farewell on Wharton's part. Lily shared some of Wharton's weaknesses, and what the 'problem-solving' process of composing this novel taught its author was that weaknesses were not viable. The conviction that a woman must necessarily be passive to be 'feminine' was banished from Wharton's life after she completed *The House of Mirth*."[40] Wharton in 1904 and 1905 was far from able to intellectualize the pain she felt at living the socially mandated life; what accrues from Wharton's own knowledge of this highly fashionable life is less her farewell to Lily as beautiful object than it is her acknowledgment that society cared nothing for such a woman. The central issue of *The House of*

Mirth becomes that realization: poignant as Lily's death may seem to the sympathetic reader of *The House of Mirth*, to her society—including her family, friends, and even possible suitors—Lily's death means nothing. That discovery of the sheer unimportance—almost irrelevance—of a beautiful woman to the whole scheme of life is the resonating knowledge of Wharton's novel. And the reader is forced to ask: If it matters to no one whether a character lives or dies, why should that character endure the struggle necessary to live?

In the months leading up to her writing this novel—so crucial for her development of herself as a professional writer—Wharton had not disguised her personal unhappiness. In the spring of 1904, she wrote to Sara Norton that the past winter had been "the dreariest" she had ever spent; she had experienced "the nervous indigestion and bad headaches which I had managed to shake off after years of misery, and I was so depressed by this return of my old ailment that I found it hard to write."[41] Given this unsettled health pattern, Wharton no doubt looked forward to the implicit "permission" given her to work every day on *The House of Mirth*, in order to meet the deadlines for its serial publication in *Scribner's*. This was the novel that made Wharton a thorough professional, and in its writing she learned that her identity as writer—and her work in that role—could circumvent, even supplant, the psychological and physiological problems that her life as a woman of society often created for her.

Wharton's relentless feelings of inferiority, of uselessness, and of constant aloneness—a psychological tapestry that led to a nearly impenetrable isolation throughout her life—gave her some incredibly moving passages in work that may not be arresting as a whole. *The House of Mirth* benefits from the tension between what Lily might achieve if society were to accept her, and what Lily feels as the rejected outcast from that society; a central paragraph in "The Fullness of Life," a story from 1893, echoes some of these feelings of distance from everything and everyone:

> I have sometimes thought that a woman's nature is like a great house full of rooms: there is the hall, through which everyone passes in going

in and out; the drawing room, where one receives formal visits; the sitting room, where the members of the family come and go as they list; but beyond that, far beyond, are other rooms, the handles of whose doors perhaps are never turned; no one knows the way to them, no one knows whither they lead; and in the innermost room, the holy of holies, the soul sits alone and waits for a footstep that never comes.[42]

It is this portion of Edith Wharton's life that she recalls, again, to Sara Norton: "How well I know those bitter times, when great trials and small inconveniences pile themselves together on the tired body and strained nerves."[43]

Had Wharton used a first-person point of view for this novel, Lily Bart might well have said something similar. But there were many reasons for Wharton's distancing the reader from Lily Bart, and one of the most important was her unwillingness to have Lily's story seen as autobiographical.[44] Therefore, to have Lily die at the end of *The House of Mirth* represents a kind of psychic risk for the author, because Wharton then faces the real terror of that aloneness and separation from others. Through her narrative strategy, Wharton makes the reader face the fact that hardly anyone cares whether Lily lives or dies. Selden uses her death to create an interesting new facade for himself—as bereaved, mourning lover. Only Gerty's involvement in sorrow seems real, and Gerty's worth has already been discounted by her atypicality throughout the book. The question that is sometimes asked by readers, "Did Lily intend to kill herself?" is of less importance than the unasked question (which Wharton's text implicitly answers), "Does anyone care whether or not Lily dies?"

In the closing years of the twentieth century, when readers have been besieged by existential texts that avoid all pretense of "answer," Lily Bart's dilemma—finding enough meaning in her life to continue her struggle for it—is all too real, and all too involving. That Wharton has presented one of the earliest depictions of women's struggle in this vacuum of firmly established meanings—the chaotic twentieth century so marked by war, political turmoil, and personal debilitation—has won for her a readership that will continue not only to read, but to assess, her work. *The House of Mirth* begins the real hegira to Wharton's full understanding of herself and her abilities, and the journey should take the reader to *The Reef* (1912), *Summer* (1917), *The Age of Innocence* (1920), *The Mother's Recompense* (1925), and *The Children* (1928). What is particularly important about *The House of Mirth* is that, rather than being any kind of an ending for Edith Wharton as writer, it becomes the first step out of what she had in 1902 called her "bloodless existence." [45] Edith Wharton, writer, was to become a compelling woman, as well as a great American modern novelist.

Notes

1. Kate Caffrey, *The 1900s Lady* (London: Gordon Cremonesi, 1976), 165.

2. Barbara Welter, *Dimity Convictions: The American Woman in the Nineteenth Century* (Athens: Ohio University Press, 1976). See also Carroll Smith-Rosenberg, "The Female World of Love and Ritual: Relations between Women in Nineteenth-Century America," *A Heritage of Her Own: Toward a New Social History of American Women*, ed. Nancy F. Cott and Elizabeth H. Pleck (New York: Simon & Schuster, 1979).

3. Barbara Ehrenreich and Deirdre English, *For Her Own Good: 150 Years of the Experts' Advice to Women* (Garden City, N.Y.: Doubleday, 1979); Elaine Showalter, *The Female Malady: Women, Madness, and English Culture, 1830–1980* (New York: Pantheon Books, 1985).

4. Ann R. Shapiro, *Unlikely Heroines: Nineteenth-Century American Women Writers and the Woman Question* (Westport, Conn.: Greenwood Press, 1987).

5. R. W. B. Lewis, *Edith Wharton: A Biography* (New York: Harper & Row, 1975), 154.

6. Cecilia Tichi, "Women Writers and the New Woman," in *Columbia Literary History of the United States,* ed. Emory Elliott (New York: Columbia University Press, 1988), 595. Tichi also points out that under the guise of being "local color" writers, many of these women were presenting truthful, if not happy, accounts of real women's lives.

7. Sandra M. Gilbert and Susan Gubar, *The Madwoman in the Attic: The Woman Writer and the Nineteenth-Century Literary Imagination* (New Haven, Conn.: Yale University Press, 1979); Rachel Blau DuPlessis, *Writing beyond the Ending: Narrative Strategies of Twentieth-Century Women Writers* (Bloomington: Indiana University Press, 1985).

8. Nina Baym, *Novels, Readers, and Reviewers* (Ithaca, N.Y.: Cornell University Press, 1984). An anonymous reviewer had written of Wharton's 1903 novel, *Sanctuary,* that it demonstrated "a beautiful, tender sentimentality

peculiar to women, whether they are writers, mothers, or missionaries" ("Edith Wharton's New Novel," *Independent* 55 [10 December 1903]: 2933-35).

9. See representative reviews in *Spectator* 95 (28 October 1905): 657; *Literary Digest* 31 (9 December 1905): 886; and *Bookman* 22 (December 1905): 364-66. The Henry James remark, as well as other information about the book's reception, appears in Lewis, *Edith Wharton*, 150-56. See also Marlene Springer, *Edith Wharton and Kate Chopin: A Reference Guide* (Boston: G. K. Hall, 1976), and Katherine Joslin, "Edith Wharton at 125," *College Literature* 14, no. 3 (1987): 193-206.

10. Reviews in *Independent* 59 (16 November 1905): 1151, 1155; *Athenaeum* (London) 4074 (25 November 1905): 718; *Atlantic Monthly* 97 (January 1906): 52-53; *Saturday Review* (London) 101 (17 February 1906): 209-10; *Bookman* (London) 29 (December 1905): 130-31.

11. "The House of Mirth," *Times Literary Supplement*, 1 December 1905, 421. Important considerations of Wharton's novel as expressing a particularly American theme are H. D. Sedgwick, "The Novels of Mrs. Wharton," *Atlantic Monthly* 98 (August 1906): 217-28; Erskine Steele, "Fiction and Social Ethics," *South Atlantic Quarterly* 5 (July 1906): 254-63; and Charles Waldstein, "Social Ideals," *North American Review* 182 (June 1906): 840-52 and 183 (July 1906): 125-36.

12. Wharton to Scribner, 11 November 1905, *The Letters of Edith Wharton*, ed. R. W. B. Lewis and Nancy Lewis (New York: Scribner's, 1988), 95.

13. Wharton to Edward L. Burlingame, 23 November 1905, *Letters*, 98.

14. Wharton to Dix, 5 December 1905, *Letters*, 99.

15. Arthur Hobson Quinn, "Edith Wharton," pamphlet, n.d., as quoted by Joslin, "Edith Wharton at 125," 205.

16. *The House of Mirth* (New York: Penguin, 1985), 3. Page numbers from this edition appear in the text subsequently.

17. Judith Fetterley, "Reading about Reading," in *Gender and Reading*, ed. Elizabeth A. Flynn and Patrocinio P. Schweickart (Baltimore: Johns Hopkins University Press, 1986), 150.

18. Frances L. Restuccia, "The Name of the Lily: Edith Wharton's Feminism(s)," *Contemporary Literature* 28 (1987): 223-38.

19. Dale M. Bauer, *Female Dialogics: A Theory of Failed Community* (Albany: State Univ. of New York Press, 1988), 126. See also Susan Gubar, "'The Blank Page' and the Issues of Female Creativity," *New Feminist Criticism*, ed. Elaine Showalter (New York: Pantheon, 1985).

20. Lewis, *Edith Wharton*, 155, 159.

21. Gilbert and Gubar, *Madwoman in the Attic*.

22. DuPlessis, *Writing beyond the Ending*, 20.

23. Several critics, most recently Alfred Bendixen in his edited collection

Notes

Haunted Women (New York: Ungar, 1985), have suggested that Wharton's real view of marriage is caught in her 1893 story "The Fullness of Life." Bendixen speculates that Wharton never reprinted this early story "possibly because its view of marriage reflected all too closely her own unhappy experience" (p. 231). The story is reprinted in *Haunted Women*, 231–42.

24. Ellen Moers, *Literary Women: The Great Writers* (Garden City, N.Y.: Doubleday, 1976); see also Elaine Showalter, *A Literature of Their Own: British Women Novelists from Bronte to Lessing* (Princeton, N.J.: Princeton University Press, 1977).

25. DuPlessis, *Writing beyond the Ending*, 42.

26. Mary Jacobus, "The Difference of View," *Women Writing and Writing about Women*, ed. Mary Jacobus (London: Croom Helm, 1979), 19–20.

27. DuPlessis, *Writing beyond the Ending*, 43.

28. Annis Pratt, *Archetypal Patterns in Women's Fiction* (Bloomington: Indiana University Press, 1981); see also DuPlessis's chapter "To 'bear my mother's name': *Kunstleromane* by Women Writers," in *Writing beyond the Ending*, 84–104.

29. DuPlessis, *Writing beyond the Ending*, 87.

30. Sandra M. Gilbert and Susan Gubar, *No Man's Land*, vol. 2, *Sexchanges* (New Haven, Conn.: Yale University Press, 1989), 139–45.

31. Henry James, *Daisy Miller* in *Daisy Miller and Other Stories*, ed. Michael Swan (New York: Penguin, 1963), 138; hereafter cited in text.

32. Henry James, *The Ambassadors* (New York: New American Library, 1960), 375.

33. Wharton to Gerhardi, 22 January 1931, from the Harry Ransom Humanities Research Center, University of Texas, Austin; used with permission of the collection.

34. Gilbert and Gubar, *No Man's Land*, vol. 2, 158.

35. *A Backward Glance* (New York: Appleton-Century, 1934), 207.

36. "A Cup of Cold Water," in *The Greater Inclination* (New York: Scribner's, 1899), 186, 196, 206.

37. *Sanctuary* (New York: Scribner's, 1903), 96.

38. Cynthia Griffin Wolff, Introduction to *The House of Mirth* (New York: Penguin, 1985), xi.

39. Lewis, *Edith Wharton*, 51.

40. Wolff, Introduction, xxvi.

41. Wharton to Norton, 5 May 1904, *Letters*, 89.

42. "The Fullness of Life" in Bendixen, *Haunted Women*, 234.

43. Wharton to Norton, 17 March 1903, *Letters*, 80.

44. Several of Edith Jones's childhood names—Lily, Rose, Pussy—are clues to the lack of distance between protagonist and author.

45. Wharton to Norton, 24 January 1902, *Letters*, 55.

Bibliography

Primary Works

Novels and Novellas

The Touchstone. New York: Scribner's, 1900.

The Valley of Decision. 2 vols. New York: Scribner's, 1902.

Sanctuary. New York: Scribner's, 1903.

The House of Mirth. New York: Scribner's, 1905.

The Fruit of the Tree. New York: Scribner's, 1907.

Madame de Treymes. New York: Scribner's, 1907.

Ethan Frome. New York: Scribner's, 1911.

The Reef. New York: Appleton, 1912.

The Custom of the Country. New York: Scribner's, 1913.

Bunner Sisters in *Xingu and Other Stories.* New York: Scribner's, 1916.

Summer. New York: Appleton, 1917.

The Marne. New York: Appleton, 1918.

The Age of Innocence. New York: Appleton, 1920.

The Glimpses of the Moon. New York: Appleton, 1922.

A Son at the Front. New York: Scribner's, 1923.

Old New York: False Dawn, The Old Maid, The Spark, New Year's Day. New York: Appleton, 1924.

The Mother's Recompense. New York: Appleton, 1925.

Twilight Sleep. New York: Appleton, 1927.

The Children. New York: Appleton, 1928.

Hudson River Bracketed. New York: Appleton, 1929.

The Gods Arrive. New York: Appleton, 1932.

The Buccaneers. New York: Appleton-Century, 1938.

Fast and Loose, a Novelette by David Olivieri. Edited by Viola Hopkins Winner. Charlottesville: University Press of Virginia, 1977. First publication of Wharton's novelette, written when she was fourteen.

Short Story Collections

The Greater Inclination. New York: Scribner's, 1899.
Crucial Instances. New York: Scribner's, 1901.
The Descent of Man and Other Stories. New York: Scribner's, 1904.
The Hermit and the Wild Woman and Other Stories. New York: Scribner's, 1908.
Tales of Men and Ghosts. New York: Scribner's, 1910.
Xingo and Other Stories. New York: Scribner's, 1916.
Here and Beyond. New York: Appleton, 1926.
Certain People. New York: Appleton, 1930.
Human Nature. New York: Appleton, 1933.
The World Over. New York: Appleton-Century, 1936.
Ghosts. New York: Appleton-Century, 1937.

Poetry

Verses. Newport, R.I.: C. E. Hammett, 1878.
Artemis to Actaeon and Other Verse. New York: Scribner's, 1909.
Twelve Poems. London: The Medici Society, 1926.

Travel Writing, Memoir, Criticism, Autobiography

The Decoration of Houses (with Ogden Codman, Jr.). New York: Scribner's, 1897.
Italian Villas and Their Gardens. New York: Century, 1904.
Italian Backgrounds. New York: Scribner's, 1905.
A Motor-Flight through France. New York: Scribner's, 1908.
Fighting France, from Dunkerque to Belfort. New York: Scribner's, 1915.
The Book of the Homeless (editor). New York: Scribner's, 1916.
French Ways and Their Meaning. New York: Appleton, 1919.
In Morocco. New York: Scribner's, 1920.
The Writing of Fiction. New York: Scribner's, 1925.
A Backward Glance. New York: Appleton-Century, 1934.

Bibliography

Translation

The Joy of Living, by Hermann Sudermann. New York: Scribner's, 1902.

Letters

The Letters of Edith Wharton. Edited by R. W. B. Lewis and Nancy Lewis. New York: Scribner's, 1988.

Secondary Works

Books

Ammons, Elizabeth. *Edith Wharton's Argument with America.* Athens: University of Georgia Press, 1980. Studies the major fiction with attention to Wharton's role as woman writer, complete with expected conflicts and disguises. An important reversal of critical trends up to this time.

Auchincloss, Louis. *Edith Wharton.* Minneapolis: University of Minnesota Press, 1961. Brief but informed critical overview.

Bauer, Dale M. *Female Dialogics: A Theory of Failed Community.* Albany: State University of New York Press, 1988. Treats *The House of Mirth* along with James's *The Golden Bowl,* Chopin's *The Awakening,* and Hawthorne's *The Blithedale Romance* using Mikhail Bakhtin's critical framework.

Bell, Millicent. *Edith Wharton and Henry James: The Story of Their Friendship.* New York: George Braziller, 1965. Using both writers' correspondence, Bell creates a full account of their relationship.

Benstock, Shari. *Women of the Left Bank: Paris, 1900–1940.* Austin: University of Texas Press, 1986. Places Wharton among a number of American women writers who emigrated to Paris, but does not do justice to Wharton's writing in this context.

Fryer, Judith. *Felicitous Space: The Imaginative Structures of Edith Wharton and Willa Cather.* Chapel Hill: University of North Carolina Press, 1986. Studies the work of each writer from the perspective of the "interconnectedness between space and the female imagination."

Gilbert, Sandra M., and Susan Gubar. *No Man's Land,* vol. 2, *Sexchanges* (New Haven, Conn.: Yale University Press, 1989). Treats Wharton's work in the context of other turn-of-the-century women writers, as well as Henry James, seeing accurately that much of Wharton's work was prompted by her anger at the conventions and traditions of literature by male writers.

Gimbel, Wendy. *Edith Wharton: Orphancy and Survival.* New York: Praeger,

1984. Reads Wharton's fiction through close parallels with her life. Special attention to the symbolic roles of houses and the development of selfhood.

Howe, Irving, ed. *Edith Wharton: A Collection of Critical Essays.* Englewood Cliffs, N.J.: Prentice-Hall, 1962. Includes Howe's essay "A Reading of *The House of Mirth,*" 119–29.

Lawson, Richard H. *Edith Wharton.* New York: Ungar, 1976. Surveys Wharton's major fiction, including some of the stories.

————. *Edith Wharton and German Literature.* Bonn: Bouvier, 1974. Explores the influence of German writers, particularly Goethe (and the bildungsroman), Nietzsche, Sudermann, and Keller. Bibliography includes criticism in German.

Lewis, R. W. B. *Edith Wharton: A Biography.* New York: Harper & Row, 1975. The thorough, authorized, prize-winning biography, which makes a substantial start at disclosing the complex woman as author. Some of Lewis's readings of the novels are dated, but this remains an important source of information about both Wharton's life and her work.

Lindberg, Gary H. *Edith Wharton and the Novel of Manners.* Charlottesville: University Press of Virginia, 1975. Discussion of Wharton's fiction as social commentary, especially *The House of Mirth, The Custom of the Country,* and *The Age of Innocence.*

Lubbock, Percy. *Portrait of Edith Wharton.* New York: Appleton-Century-Crofts, 1947. Informal memoir, not meant to be impartial.

Lyde, Marilyn. *Edith Wharton: Convention and Morality in the Work of a Novelist.* Norman: Oklahoma University Press, 1959. Focuses on Wharton's changing social conventions in relation to her moral philosophy.

McDowell, Margaret. *Edith Wharton.* Boston: Twayne, 1976. Good close study of Wharton's fiction, which includes the necessary biographical facts applied in reasonable ways. Sees that Wharton was continually experimenting technically.

Nevius, Blake. *Edith Wharton: A Study of Her Fiction.* Berkeley: University of California Press, 1961. First major study of Wharton's fiction, emphasizing her interest in her characters' need to choose between individual freedom and social responsibility.

Rae, Catherine M. *Edith Wharton's New York Quartet.* Lanham, Md.: University Press of America, 1984. Reading of the four novellas (*False Dawn, The Old Maid, New Year's Day,* and *The Spark*) that comprise this sometimes-overlooked but important work.

Saunders, Catherine E. *Writing the Margins: Edith Wharton, Ellen Glasgow, and the Literary Tradition of the Ruined Woman* (English Honors Essay, 1986). Cambridge, Mass.: English Department, Harvard University, 1987. Textual study of fiction by Glasgow and Wharton, finding the former's work more aggressively critical of society and women's place in it.

Bibliography

Schriber, Mary Suzanne. *Gender and the Writer's Imagination: From Cooper to Wharton*. Lexington: University Press of Kentucky, 1987. Studies cultural stereotypes of women's roles in works by Cooper, Hawthorne, Howells, James, and Wharton; in the later work of Wharton, Schriber finds interesting use made of concepts of women's sexuality.

Stein, Allen F. *After the Vows Were Spoken: Marriage in American Literary Realism*. Columbus: Ohio State University Press, 1984. Includes three chapters on Wharton's fiction, studying her depiction of marriage as entrapment, as less than ideal, and as a means to moral growth.

Walton, Geoffrey. *Edith Wharton: A Critical Introduction*. 2d ed. Rutherford, N.J.: Fairleigh Dickinson University Press, 1982. Detailed and general substantial interpretations of Wharton's fiction.

Wershoven, Carol. *The Female Intruder in the Novels of Edith Wharton*. Rutherford, N.J.: Fairleigh Dickinson University Press, 1982. Sets up four patterns for Wharton's use of a strong female character, the "intruder," an outsider who criticizes social norms and brings more positive values to the culture.

Wolff, Cynthia Griffin. *A Feast of Words: The Triumph of Edith Wharton*. New York: Oxford University Press, 1977. Making extensive use of psychoanalytical insights, this study of Wharton's work includes the fiction's relationship to the author's life and experiences as a woman. Detailed readings of the novels and the "Beatrice Palmetto" fragment.

Essays

Ammons, Elizabeth. "Cool Diana and the Blood-Red Muse: Edith Wharton on Innocence and Art." In *American Novelists Revisited: Essays in Feminist Criticism*, edited by Fritz Fleischmann, 209–24. Boston: G. K. Hall, 1982.

Auchincloss, Louis. "Edith Wharton." In *American Writers: A Collection of Literary Biographies*, edited by Leonard Unger. New York: Scribner's, 1974.

Barnett, Louise K. "American Novelists and the 'Portrait of Beatrice Cenci.'" *New England Quarterly* 53 (1980): 168–83.

Beaty, Robin. "'Lilies that Fester': Sentimentality in *The House of Mirth*." *College Literature* 14 (1987): 263–74. Complete issue on Wharton.

Blum, Virginia L. "Edith Wharton's Erotic Other World." *Literature and Psychology* 33 (1987): 12–29.

Brazin, Nancy Topping. "The Destruction of Lily Bart: Capitalism, Christianity, and Male Chauvinism." *Denver Quarterly* 17 (1983): 97–108.

Collinson, C. W. "The Whirlpool and *The House of Mirth*." *Gissing Newsletter* 16 (1980): 12–16.

Coard, Robert L. "Names in the Fiction of Edith Wharton." *Names* 13 (1965): 1-10.

Cuddy, Lois A. "Triangles of Defeat and Liberation: The Quest for Power in Edith Wharton's Fiction." *Perspectives on Contemporary Literature* 8 (1982): 18-26.

Dahl, Curtis. "Edith Wharton's *The House of Mirth:* Sermon on a Text." *Modern Fiction Studies* 21 (1975): 572-76.

Davidson, Cathy N. "Kept Women in *The House of Mirth.*" *Markham Review* 9 (1979): 10-13.

Dimock, Wai-chee. "Debasing Exchange: Edith Wharton's *The House of Mirth.*" *PMLA* 100 (1985): 783-92.

Dixon, Roslyn. "Reflecting Vision in *The House of Mirth.*" *Twentieth Century Literature* 33 (1987): 211-22.

Fetterley, Judith. "'The Temptation to be a Beautiful Object': Double Standard and Double Bind in *The House of Mirth.*" *Studies in American Fiction* 5 (1977): 199-211.

French, Marilyn. Introduction to *The House of Mirth.* New York: Berkeley, 1981.

————. "Muzzled Women." *College Literature* 14 (1987): 219-29.

Hays, Peter L. "Bearding the Lily: Wharton's Names." *American Notes and Queries* 18 (1980): 75-76.

Joslin, Katherine. "Edith Wharton at 125." *College Literature* 14 (1987): 193-206.

Kaplan, Amy. "Edith Wharton's Profession of Authorship." *ELH* 53 (1986): 433-57.

Karcher, Carolyn L. "Male Vision and Female Revision in James's *Wings of the Dove* and Wharton's *The House of Mirth.*" *Women's Studies* 10 (1984): 227-44.

Koprince, Susan. "The Meaning of Bellomont in *The House of Mirth.*" *Edith Wharton Newsletter* 2 (1985): 2.

Langley, Martha R. "Botanical Language in Edith Wharton's *The House of Mirth.*" *Notes on Modern American Literature* 5 (1980): item 3.

Lidoff, Joan. "Another Sleeping Beauty: Narcissism in *The House of Mirth.*" *American Quarterly* 32 (1980): 519-39. Reprinted in *American Realism: New Essays,* edited by Eric J. Sundquist. Baltimore: Johns Hopkins University Press, 1982.

Michaelson, Bruce. "Edith Wharton's House Divided." *Studies in American Fiction* 12 (1984): 199-215.

Miller, Carol. "'Natural Magic': Irony as Unifying Strategy in *The House of Mirth.*" *South Central Review* 4 (1987): 82-91.

O'Neal, Michael J. "Point of View and Narrative Technique in the Fiction of Edith Wharton." *Style* 17 (1983): 270-89.

Pickrel, Paul. "*Vanity Fair* in America: *The House of Mirth* and *Gone with the Wind.*" *American Literature* 59 (1987): 37-57.

Bibliography

Poirier, Richard. "Edith Wharton, *The House of Mirth*." In *The American Novel from James Fenimore Cooper to William Faulkner,* edited by Wallace Stegner, 117–32. New York: Basic Books, 1965.

Price, Alan. "Lily Bart and Carrie Meeber: Cultural Sisters." *American Literary Realism* 13 (1980): 238–45.

Restuccia, Frances L. "The Name of the Lily: Edith Wharton's Feminism(s)." *Contemporary Literature* 28 (1987): 223–38.

Rideout, Walter B. "Edith Wharton's *The House of Mirth*." In *Twelve Original Essays on Great American Novels,* edited by Charles Shapiro, 148–76. Detroit: Wayne State University Press, 1958.

Rooke, Constance. "Beauty in Distress: *Daniel Deronda* and *The House of Mirth*." *Women and Literature* 4 (1976): 28–39.

Schriber, Mary Suzanne. "Convention in the Fiction of Edith Wharton." *Studies in American Fiction* 11 (1983): 189–201.

Showalter, Elaine. "The Death of the Lady (Novelist): Wharton's *The House of Mirth*." *Representations* 9 (1985): 133–49.

Shulman, Robert. "Divided Selves and the Market Society: Politics and Psychology in *The House of Mirth*." *Perspectives on Contemporary Literature* 11 (1985): 10–19.

Spangler, George M. "Suicide and Social Criticism: Durkeim, Dreiser, Wharton, and London." *American Quarterly* 31 (1980): 496–516.

Stineback, David C. "'The whirling surfaces of existence': Edith Wharton's *The House of Mirth* (1905)." In *Shifting World: Social Change and Nostalgia in the American Novel.* Lewisburg, Pa.: Bucknell University Press, 1976.

Westbrook, Wayne W. "Lily—Bartering on the New York Social Exchange in *The House of Mirth*." *Ball State University Forum* 20 (1979): 59–64.

————. "*The House of Mirth* and the Insurance Scandal of 1905." *American Notes and Queries* 14 (1976): 134–37.

Wolff, Cynthia Griffin, "Lily Bart and the Beautiful Death." *American Literature* 46 (1974): 36–40.

————. Introduction to *The House of Mirth*. New York: Penguin Books, 1985.

Zilversmit, Annette. "Edith Wharton's Last Ghosts." *College Literature* 14 (1987): 296–305.

Bibliographies

Bendixen, Alfred. "A Guide to Wharton Criticism, 1976–1983." *Edith Wharton Newsletter* 2 (1985): 1–8. Entire issue.

————. "Recent Wharton Studies: A Bibliographic Essay." *Edith Wharton Newsletter* 3 (1986): 5, 8–9.

————. "Wharton Studies, 1986–1987: A Bibliographic Essay." *Edith Wharton Newsletter* 5 (1988): 5–8, 10.

Brenni, Vito J. *Edith Wharton: A Bibliography.* Morgantown, Va.: McClain Printing Co., 1966.

Schriber, Mary Suzanne. "Edith Wharton and the French Critics, 1906–1937." *American Literary Realism* 13 (1980): 61–72.

Springer, Marlene. *Edith Wharton and Kate Chopin: A Reference Guide.* Boston: G. K. Hall, 1976.

Tuttleton, James W. "Edith Wharton." In *American Women Writers: Bibliographical Essays,* edited by Maurice Duke, Jackson R. Bryer, and M. Thomas Inge, 71–107. Westport, Conn.: Greenwood Press, 1983. Updates Tuttleton's original essay in *Resources for American Literary Study* 3 (1973).

Zilversmit, Annette. "Appendix, Bibliographical Index." *College Literature* 14 (1987): 305–9.

Index

Alcott, Louisa May: *Work*, 6
American Girl, The, 5–6, 29, 66, 68–69
Anderson, Sherwood: *Winesburg, Ohio*, 10
Athenaeum, The (London), 9
"anxiety of authorship," 7

Bauer, Dale M., 39
Baym, Nina: *Novels, Readers, and Reviewers*, 8

Chopin, Kate, 2, 6, 7, 54, 67; *Awakening, The*, 2, 6, 7, 54, 67; *Bayou Folk*, 6

Daisy Miller. See James, Henry
Declaration of Sentiments and Resolutions, The, 2–3
Dix, Morgan, 10–11
Dixon, Thomas: *The Clansman*, 5
Dreiser, Theodore: *Sister Carrie*, 6
DuPlessis, Rachel Blau, 49–50, 53, 55, 56; *Writing Beyond the Ending: Narrative Strategies of Twentieth-Century Women Writers*, 49–50

Eliot, George, 5, 9; *Middlemarch*, 5; *Mill on the Floss, The*, 5

Faulkner, William: *Sartoris*, 10
Fields, Annie, 10
Fitzgerald, F. Scott, 7

Flaubert, Gustave: *Madame Bovary*, 5
Freeman, Mary Wilkins: *New England Nun, A*, 6
Fuller, Margaret, 2

Gerhardi, William, 75
Gilbert, Sandra M., 7, 49, 66–67
Gilman, Charlotte Perkins, 3, 6, 7, 67; *Women and Economics*, 3, 6, 67; "Yellow Wallpaper, The," 6, 7
Glasgow, Ellen, 9
Grimke, Sarah: *Letters on the Equality of the Sexes and the Condition of Women*, 2
Gubar, Susan, 7, 49, 66–67

Haggard, Rider: *She*, 67
Hardy, Thomas: *Tess of the D'Urbervilles*, 5
Hichan, Robert Smythe: *The Garden of Allah*, 5

Ibsen, Hendrik, 2, 5; *Doll's House, A*, 2, 5; *Hedda Gabler*, 5
International Council of Women, 1888, 3

Jacobus, Mary, 54
James, Henry, 5–6, 9, 66–76; *Ambassadors, The*, 66, 74–75; *American, The*, 66; *Daisy Miller*, 5, 66–76; *Golden Bowl, The*, 66; *Portrait of a Lady*,

The, 6, 66; *Roderick Hudson*, 66; *Wings of the Dove, The*, 66
Jane Eyre, 67
Jewett, Sarah Orne, 6, 10; *Country of the Pointed Firs, The*, 6
Jones, Edith. *See* Wharton, Edith
Jones, Lucretia (Edith Wharton's mother), 85

Lessing, Doris: *Four-Gated City, The*, 55
Lewis, R.W. B., 85

Madwoman in the Attic: The Woman Writer and the Nineteenth Century Literary Imagination, The, 49
Martineau, Harriet, 2
Maupassant, Guy de, 9
Meynell, Alice, 9
Moers, Ellen, 53
Moss, Mary, 9
Mott, Lucretia, 2

New Woman, 1–3, 5, 6
Norton, Sara, 40, 86, 87

Pratt, Annis, 55

Quinn, Arthur Hobson, 11

Restuccia, Frances, 33–34

Saturday Review (London), 9
Schreiner, Olive: *Story of an African Farm, The*, 67
Scribner, Charles, 10
Scribner's, 76
Scribner's, 5, 86
Seneca Falls Convention, 1848, 2–3
Sinclair, Upton: *Jungle, The*, 5
Stanton, Elizabeth Cady, 2, 3
Stein, Gertrude, 3
Stevens, Harry, 85
Sturgis, Howard, 9

Tarkington, Booth, 9
Times Literary Supplement, 9

Tolstoy, Leo: *Anna Karenina*, 5
True Woman, 3–4

Veblen, Thorstein: *Theory of the Leisure Class, The*, 67

Ward, Elizabeth Stuart Phelps: *Silent Partner, The* and *Story of Avis, The*, 6
Wharton, Edith, 1, 3, 6–7, 8–88; as New Woman, 1; life in fiction, 1, 53–54, 74–76, 84–88; on marriage, 75; on the moral purpose of fiction, 10–11

PROSE WORKS:
Age of Innocence, The, 88
Backward Glance, A, 77
Children, The, 88
Crucial Instances, 8
"Cup of Cold Water, A," 82–83
Descent of Man and Other Stories, The, 8
"Fullness of Life, The," 86–87
Greater Inclination, The, 8

HOUSE OF MIRTH, THE, 3–4, 6–88; "A Moment's Ornament," 25; "The Year of the Rose," 82; anti-Semitism, 61; as *bildungsroman*, 32, 55; as domestic novel, 51, 54; as *kunstlerroman*, 55; as novel of manners, 6, 24, 77; as novel of marriage, 25, 50, 54, 56, 58, 64; as quest novel, 55; humor in, 10; irony, 3, 15, 21, 24, 30, 50, 52, 63, 67, 83–84; point of view in, 15–29; structure of, 30–40; subtext of, 7, 49–57

Characters in:
Bart, Lily, 3–4, 5, 8–9, 11, 15–21, 22–28
Dorset, Bertha, 19–21, 33, 35, 46, 59, 62–64, 67, 71–72, 82
Farish, Gerty, 18, 21, 22–26, 41, 47, 53, 54, 56–57, 64, 73, 78, 87
Peniston, Julia, 18–20, 26, 29, 35, 42, 45–46, 52, 53–55, 79

Index

Selden, Lawrence, 6–7, 9, 15–21, 23–28, 30–40, 43–44, 50–52, 54–56, 58–64, 68–75, 78, 82–84, 87

Mother's Recompense, The, 88
Reef, The, 88
Sanctuary, 8, 82, 83

Summer, 88
Touchstone, The, 8
Valley of Decision, The, 8

Wharton, Teddy, 85
Wolff, Cynthia Griffen, 85
Woolf, Virginia: *To the Lighthouse,* 55

About the Author

Linda Wagner-Martin is Hanes Professor of English at the University of North Carolina, Chapel Hill. Her most recent books are *Sylvia Plath: A Biography*, *Critical Essays on Anne Sexton*, and *The Modern American Novel, 1914–1945*. She has written widely on such American authors as Ernest Hemingway, Ellen Glasgow, John Dos Passos, William Faulkner, Robert Frost, William Carlos Williams, and Denise Levertov. A former editor of the *Centennial Review*, she has taught at Bowling Green State University, Wayne State University, and Michigan State University and has been a Guggenheim and a Bunting Institute fellow.